COLUMBIA TUSCULUM

A History of Cincinnati's Oldest Neighborhood

DINESE YOUNG

THE
History
PRESS

Published by The History Press
Charleston, SC
www.historypress.com

Back cover: Modern image of the Carnegie Center of Columbia Tusculum, once East End Library. *Tim Jeffries, Moving Pictures Photography.*

Opposite: The CG&P ticket office was located on Carrel Street. *Vickie Rafferty.*

First published 2024

Manufactured in the United States

ISBN 9781467158558

Library of Congress Control Number: 2024938202

This book is dedicated to the residents and volunteers who have donated much to preserve, grow and develop the community's history, architecture and social fabric. The diversity of community residents, their interactions with one another and contributions to the community are what give character to a neighborhood, and Columbia Tusculum's character is as enduring as the river's current.

Additionally, this book is dedicated to my amazing family—Ben, Sophia, Eloise and William—whose love, loyalty and support are the most valuable resources in my life.

CONTENTS

ACKNOWLEDGEMENTS

This book owes its existence to the collaborative efforts of a supportive community. Numerous individuals graciously contributed their archives, histories, time and resources, essential elements without which the publication would not have been possible. The book's primary objective is to centralize and disseminate the community's photos, archives and histories, historically held in private hands, to make them accessible to a broader audience.

The inspiration for this project stemmed from the research conducted in 1988 by former residents Mary Ann Knoop, Brenda Lugar and Bonnie Schneider, all of whom were dedicated to preserving the community's legacy in celebration of its two-hundred-year anniversary. Their diligent efforts laid the foundation for an updated and extended community history. Thirty-six years later, this book seeks a new audience to continue their passion of historic preservation.

Special gratitude is extended to St. Stephens Catholic Church, Aston Allen of Mount Carmel Baptist Church and Steve Ham of Grace and Truth Cincinnati Baptist for generously sharing their extensive archives and resources. Steve's generosity, allowing access during a hectic move to a new building, was particularly noteworthy. Linda Wedding, a descendant of Benjamin Stites, shared a wealth of family stories and history, sufficient to fill a book of her own. Courtney Pegan's passionate and detailed research helped with several home histories, including 3710 and 3631 Morris Place and 315 and 317 Tusculum Avenue.

Linda Wedding is the great-great-great-granddaughter of Major Benjamin Stites. Her mother was Estella Stites, and her father was Russell Stites; his father was Henry Stites, son of William Stites. William was Major Benjamin Stites's son with Hannah Waring. Linda portrays Hannah in "1788 Revisited," now at Heritage Village Museum. Linda continues the legacy of her grandfather Russell Stites by caring for Pioneer Cemetery and sharing its legacy.

The inclusion of beautiful vintage photos is also credited to Vicki Rafferty, Laura Joppru, Janette Jackson and Brian Williams, among others. Williams is specially recognized for creating a remarkable community Facebook site ("Cincinnati's East End, Columbia Tusculum & Linwood"), fostering the sharing of abundant vintage community photos and stories among current and past residents. Special acknowledgments go to J. Michael Smith of Yeatman Lodge and Jenn Schafer of the Junior League of Cincinnati for sharing their histories and filling in crucial missing links. Jeb Portman's extensive research on the Morris House was invaluable, as there are many mixed and conflicting details about its past.

Four generations of Vicki's family were from the Columbia Tusculum neighborhood. Her grandfather was the station agent for the Carrel St. Depot of the CG&P, and her great-great-grandfather W.T. Matthews was the stationmaster at the Little Miami railroad station, where her great-grandmother Mary Jane Matthews worked as a telegraph operator. The man she married, John C. Kemmeter, also worked for the railroad, as did her step-uncle, Benjamin Dudley. Her great-great-great-grandparents William Matthews and Margaret Caster Matthews Dudley are buried at the Pioneer Cemetery along with two of their grandsons, Cecil Osborn Matthews and Southtown McCullough Matthews. The men belonged to the Odd Fellows, who held meetings in Spencer Township Hall.

Lastly, I dedicate this book to my family. Heartfelt thanks are extended to Sophia Young, my talented daughter, for her invaluable writing feedback and creative assistance. The unwavering support, patience and encouragement from my entire family (Ben, Sophia, Eloise and William) throughout the lengthy publishing process are deeply appreciated—they inspire me every day. This book is a testament for them to never give up on goals, no matter the time, effort or obstacles that hinder completion.

NOTE FROM AUTHOR

The history of a community does not commence upon the arrival of white settlers, although it may seem like such when researching historical texts. This book is not an exhaustive history and acknowledges the immense holes in time and perspective from the many Native Americans who lived their lives on the same river bottomland for at least two thousand years prior to the arrival of white settlers.

Throughout the many historic texts, documents and artifacts researched for this book, an almost completely one-sided perspective from settlers was represented when describing firsthand accounts and situations during the early years of Columbia. Like most, these settlers were likely unaware of the long, complex history Natives in the area had with white European traders and soldiers prior to the first permanent settlement, which would explain the fluctuation and complexity of their responses to and interactions with the settlers. When hearing only one perspective, it is easy to understand and empathize with that lived experience. However, Native American history, experiences and perspectives were rarely recorded in writing, and if they were, it was usually by or through white hands that likely added interpretation and bias.

There is much about what Natives thought, lived and experienced both prior to the arrival of white settlers and then after the permanent white communities expanded and pushed them out that we still do not know. While there may be a lack of quantity and quality of written Native histories, I encourage readers searching for a more extensive and encompassing history of all cultures who lived in land now known as Cincinnati to explore the following resources:

Myaamia Center at Miami University
Bonham House
351 East Spring Street
Oxford, OH 45056
https://miamioh.edu/myaamia-center/index.html

The Miami Tribe of Oklahoma
Miami Nation Headquarters
3410 P Street NW
Miami, OK 74354
https://miamination.com

The Shawnee Tribe
29 South Highway 69A
Miami, OK 74354
https://shawnee-nsn.gov

Ohio's Prehistoric Past
Hopewell Culture National Historic Park
16062 OH-104
Chillicothe, OH 45601
https://www.nps.gov/articles/000/ohio-s-prehistoric-past.htm

The story of any community includes a broad timeline not easily encompassed in a singular book. However, all communities and cultures across time flourished in the location now known as Columbia Tusculum due to the vitality of the river basin and life sources it provided that all communities needed to thrive—water, transportation, food, lush soil for agriculture, proximity to other communities and more. The Ohio River has always anchored humans to this area and continues to fuel human progress over time.

INTRODUCTION

The Little Miami River makes a fishing hook U-turn and pours into the rushing Ohio River. Above this point, there is a sudden bend where the community of Columbia Tusculum situates like a fish caught in a net. Like many river towns, Columbia's history, livelihood, progress and even struggles have been tied to the ribbon of water rushing past on its race to the Mississippi. It's a community that everyone has passed if they have traveled from downtown to an eastern neighborhood, although few know its importance in the anchoring and development of the city of Cincinnati. The very first permanent Anglo-American settlement in what became southwest Ohio and only second in the Northwest Territory, it not only is Cincinnati's oldest neighborhood, but it is also an area that has always been a thoroughfare of people and goods east of the city.

Prior to the white settlers, Native tribes also used this location for their communities and trade routes for hundreds of years. It is a neighborhood where evolution and change are necessary for survival, and it has shed its old skin many times to redefine itself with changing times and migrations of people. This book explores some of the rich history of Columbia Tusculum, and the reader is invited to discover the neighborhood whose roots are pivotal to Cincinnati's own. No matter what changes take place in the culture, transportation and economy of Cincinnati, Columbia Tusculum will continue to evolve and connect community through time.

NATIVE AMERICANS

Southwest Ohio's history dates to least two thousand years ago, when peaceful Mound Builders were the sole human inhabitants of the area. Around AD 1600, they mysteriously disappeared, possibly due to disease or hostile tribe invasions. White Europeans first discovered the area with Robert LaSalle's expedition in 1682 down the Ohio River. He was so impressed by the beauty of the land that he nicknamed it La Belle Riviere (the Beautiful River) and claimed the land for France. However, France had no interest in settling the land. Profitable fur trading did quickly develop between Europeans and Natives in the Ohio River Valley, which created a tenuous relationship between them. Ancient burial mounds were found throughout the area, with many in the adjacent community of Linwood.

Ohio was considered "original Indian Territory" to the United States in the 1790s. When other Indigenous nations were forced into conflict or relocation, Ohio was one of the areas to which they migrated. In the early 1700s, several Native tribes migrated to the Ohio River Valley—including Seneca, Miami, Shawnee, Ottawa, Lenape (Delaware) and Wyandot—drawn by fertile farmlands and ample game for hunting. Several other tribes migrated in and out of Ohio, but these five represent the most predominant Indigenous populations. The two main tribes in the southwest region of Ohio where Columbia and Cincinnati were established were the Miami and Shawnee.

The Miami tribe called themselves the Myaamia in their Algonquian language, which translates to "the downstream people," and they were one of the main tribes occupying the area surrounding what is now known as Cincinnati. They were excellent hunters of white-tailed deer, were slow-spoken and polite. Myaamia were among those nations exposed to early European contact, first through the Jesuit mission in the late 1600s, followed soon after by the French and British invasion and struggle for control of the Great Lakes region. The Myaamia people enjoyed elaborate dress and tattooing. Their tribe was originally present in northern Indiana, but the presence of British military pushed them farther south, where they were well settled in the southwest Ohio territory during the late 1700s. The Myaamia endured hardships of disease, war and colonization as well and were eventually forced to relocate to Kansas and then Oklahoma. The Treaty of Greenville in 1795 was the first treaty this tribe entered with the American government, and the Treaty of Mississine, signed in 1826, took away most of the Miami lands. Modern-day Miami tribes are in Indiana and Oklahoma.

Shawnee was a tribe dominant in southwest Ohio whose experiences with whites dated back to the 1600s. They were an Algonquian-speaking tribe, and their name comes from the Algonquian word *shawun*, meaning "southerner," and reference their original location in the Ohio Valley. In 1682, the Shawnee in Ohio and Pennsylvania entered their first peace treaty with whites with Quaker William Penn. The Shawnee traveled great distances to trade and hunt and were known to be devoted friends as well as fierce foes. One Quaker minister in 1706 was shocked to find women regularly a part of the Shawnee councils and active in decision-making on behalf of the tribe. In the 1730s, the Shawnee were back in the Ohio region. Before 1754, the Shawnee still had a stronghold in Virginia but moved west across the Alleghenies as they were pushed out by white settlers. The Shawnee first became allies of the French in the French and Indian War (1754–63) until switching sides to support the British in 1758. The reason for the switch was that in exchange for rights to Shawnee hunting grounds, the British promised to not colonize west of the Alleghany Mountains, thus protecting Shawnee territories from white settlement. This allegiance with the British continued throughout and past the American Revolution, when Shawnee fought with the British in hopes to prevent settlement farther west from colonies. They were active in the Northwest Indian Wars in the 1790s and even participated in the War of 1812 between the British and Americans. The Canadian British were believed to have encouraged Native Americans in the territory to attack American settlements to disrupt and weaken their hold on the area.

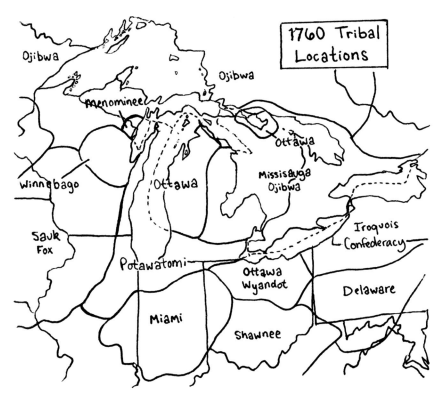

This map shows 1760 Native tribal locations in what would later be known as the Northwest Territory. *Sophia Young.*

The Shawnee ultimately migrated into western states such as Missouri, Arkansas and Kansas. Today, there are three federally recognized tribes of Shawnee People in Oklahoma: Absentee-Shawnee, Loyal Shawnee (Shawnee Tribe of Oklahoma) and Eastern Shawnee.

When the Americans won their independence from Great Britain in 1783, with the Treaty of Paris ending the American Revolution, the Northwest Territory became the property of America. This led to the creation of the Northwest Ordinance on July 13, 1787, which outlined steps for regions in the Northwest Territory to become states, thereby expanding the country. This necessitated migration of white settlers into the territory, so land was sold for as cheap as one dollar per acre. The cost, in addition to abundant game and fertile soil, enticed many soldiers just out of war and looking to settle down. Unfortunately, these plans for expansion and development were made without any consideration of the multiple tribes of Natives already occupying the region or their already simmering and residual feelings from decades of conflict with white soldiers and manipulative treaties. This ultimately led to conflict and resistance from tribes who initially welcomed trade with new settlers.

Both the Shawnee, led by Blue Jacket, as well as the Myaamia, led by Little Turtle, were active in the Northwest Indian Wars in the 1790s. Fighting culminated in 1794 when the Alliance was defeated by General "Mad" Anthony Wayne at the Battle of Fallen Timbers, resulting in, after months of negotiation, representatives from the Shawnee and ten other tribes signing the Treaty of Greenville, which required natives to forfeit their lands in the Ohio Territory. After the Treaty of Greenville, Natives no longer were a considered a threat, so white settlers poured into the southwest Ohio region, leading to the rapid growth of Columbia, Cincinnati and other settlements in the region. However, the treaty did not completely dispel resentment, tension and conflict between Natives and settlers over the next twenty years.

The Greenville Treaty, however, granted a collective of European settlers' legal permission to claim Ohio as farmland. With the succession of wars and the American Revolution from 1747 to 1794, many settlers seized the opportunity to obtain cheap and available land, seeking after their own prosperity. From that point on, the Indigenous communities in Ohio either left or remained unrecognized. Treaties eventually culminated in the Ohio Removal of Native Americans between 1840 and 1845, which is sometimes referred to as the second Trail of Tears. However, many Indigenous people remained in Ohio after the removal, refusing to move west and being declared no longer Indian by the U.S. government. This led to record falsification on identities, with about half of all living Indigenous Americans in the United States lacking identity cards.

The land between the modern-day Big Miami and Little Miami Rivers became known as the "Miami Slaughterhouse" because of the ferocity between the tribes and with settlers. This area was a thoroughfare for multiple tribes' hunting and trading expeditions into Kentucky. This also was the exact area where white settlers first came to colonize southwest Ohio, landing in a contentious and prized region by Natives whose history with whites was already extensive and distrustful. Major Benjamin Stites led a party of settlers down the Ohio River to form the first permanent white settlement in Southwest Ohio and the second in the Northwest Territory in November 1788.

Native Americans initially observed Major Benjamin Stites's party on the banks of the Ohio River across from their first blockhouse. Their hunting

Lowlands along Little Miami River as seen here were known as Turkey Bottoms, later Lunken Airport, at the time of Emry Riddle Company. *Brian Williams.*

camp was six miles from the river, and they returned to hold a council deciding to approach the settlers as friends. A white man named George had been living with the Natives for ten years or more and could speak both languages. It was decided that he and one other Native would approach the blockhouse and call for their attention and engagement. However, the settlers mistook him as a member of their group, did not pay attention to his initiations and asked him why he wouldn't approach if George wanted to talk. George and the Native returned discouraged to the hunting camp and gathered a party of five Natives armed and on horses. Upon their return to the blockhouse, the group stumbled on three men surveying who were alarmed at their sight. A Native took off his cap, lowered his gun and held out his right hand as a token of friendship. George called out to the other party not to fire, as the Indians were their friends, and did not wish to hurt them, and they would like to be led to the blockhouse.

Now on friendly terms, the settlers led the Natives to meet Major Stites. The joint arrival surprised the settlement, whose residents worried that Natives were there to spy and calculate their fortifications and defenses. However, both groups began to form sociable neighbor relations where there was considerable friendliness. Some whites even frequently visited and spent nights at the Native camps, and the Natives in turn spent days and nights in Columbia, especially to trade for and drink whiskey. The Natives particularly enjoyed visiting Judge Symmes because he saved one of their small camps from the Kentuckians during the surveying expedition the year before. During the first winter in Columbia, food was scarce, and corn given to them by the Natives helped them survive until they could plant and harvest their summer crops.

The initially welcoming Natives did not yet realize the great mobilization of settlers to the Northwest Territory, although they were not inexperienced with less pleasant interactions from trade and battles with French and British soldiers. After realizing the expanding and permanent presence of soldiers at Fort Washington downstream, Natives became nervous and distrustful of all new residents.

Furthering the change in attitude toward the settlers is the implied feeling of unfair or inequitable trading between Natives and white merchants. William Goforth opened the first village store in 1789 and noted in his books that on April 21, 1789, the first Native Americans came to trade. Because of limited competition, price gauging became common. Reverend John Smith even owned a store that made 100 percent profit on everything he sold. Natives were known to steal things to even a trade they deemed inequitable, including but not limited to horses. This was seen as a provocation and attack by settlers instead of a debt being settled, as was the intent of the Natives. In fact, in April 1789, just months after the amiable Christmas celebration, the Natives stole horses on their way back to their spring camp, which left the settlers angry and without horses for spring plowing and other labor.

From an alternative perspective, John Cleves Symmes wrote about the account that represents the unfair trades that fueled these retaliations on settlers:

> *Those Indians which had continued in the neighborhood of Columbia all this while moved off about the same time, not without being offended by the treatment they met from the traders who came down the Ohio with whisky and some other articles. They had sold the Indians whiskey which had been frozen in the cask before they reached their camp: they made an Indian path for a rifle gun 30, the Indians say 40, bucks, which they valued at $1 each, besides a horse of $15 in price. A worthless gunsmith who undertook to put a new chop worth one-and-sixpence—for the flint—to the cock on an Indian's rifle, made the Indian leave two bucks for the work before he would undertake it: and another Indian, calling for the gun, was forced to pay two bucks more before the smith would give up the gun. This ill-usage the Indians complained of very*

much: the consequence was that in a very short time after the Indians
left Columbia several of the horses were stolen from Columbia. When a
party under command of Lieutenant Bailey went in pursuit of the felons.

Symmes's letter continues at length regarding a spirit of fairness in how the horses were stolen back by the whites in retaliation and the Indians came in and compromised matters in the end.

With the growing presence of soldiers, expansion of Fort Washington and trade conflicts, tensions grew and attacks on settlers increased to a near constant state of conflict. Natives were known to capture settlers, including one adolescent boy named Oliver Spencer who later wrote a memoir about the experience. Many captives were adopted into Native tribes and families, and others were used as hostages to trade with the government. The eventual attitude of the settlers against the Natives became so strong that they offered to pay $30 per Native scalp. In 1794, William Brown, one of the two original Purple Heart recipients and a Columbia settler, headed a committee fund for residents of Columbia and Cincinnati providing $135 for the "first ten Indian scalps with right ear appendage" to frighten Natives and reduce attacks on within the white settlements despite engaging in the same activities labeled "barbaric" by whites. Columbia Baptist Church required members to carry guns to Sunday service due to fear of the Natives attacking. This warlike state lasted until General Anthony Wayne's army defeated the Native tribes in 1794 at the Battle of Fallen Timbers, which ultimately led to the removal of Natives from their lands.

Ultimately, the battles and treaties pushed Natives out of Ohio, changing forever the lives of Native tribes and increasing growth of white settlements in southwest Ohio, which ultimately turned into the bustling city of Cincinnati. Ohio quickly became a state in 1803.

FOUNDING OF COLUMBIA

The lush lands of what is modernly known as Ohio have been home to Natives of various tribes and affiliations dating back to prehistoric times. Some of these were transient and others much more established and long-term communities. However, Cincinnati's inception as a city in the U.S. government and eventual state of Ohio begins with twenty-six white settlers led by a Revolutionary War veteran by the name of Benjamin Stites. In 1897, Congress established the Northwest Ordinance, which created the United States' first incorporated territory, the Northwest Territory, and opened the land for settlement. This land was acquired from the British government in the Treaty of Paris of 1783, which ended the Revolutionary War. It was land necessary to pursue the U.S. government's goal of westward expansion, as the British government had tried to block expansion of white settlement west of the Appalachian Mountains. The territory included land west of Pennsylvania, east of the Mississippi River and northwest of the Ohio River and covered all current states of Ohio, Indiana, Illinois, Michigan and Wisconsin, as well as parts of modern-day Minnesota and Indiana.

Benjamin Stites was born in 1734 in Scotch Plains, New Jersey, and died in Columbia on August 30, 1804. He took an active part in border warfare in Western Pennsylvania during the Revolutionary War. After the war, he was working as a tradesman along the Ohio River, and in the spring of 1787, he descended the Ohio in a flatboat on a trading expedition, landing at Limestone, Kentucky, present-day Maysville, which was a settlement of fifteen families. Those families were not in need of the goods Stites was

The first house built in Cincinnati was on Front east of Main. *Grace and Truth Church.*

selling, so he ventured back up the Ohio to Washington, Kentucky, to trade. While there, he heard the settlers talking of the Natives from northern Ohio recently crossing the Ohio and stealing their horses. They were concerned of the potential for continued theft and risk to their essential livestock. Explaining his extensive experience in warfare with the Natives, Stites convinced the group to take a few men and go after the thieves to retrieve the horses. Since Stites was not only convincing but also described as a tall, strong man in his fifties, the settlers agreed to the expedition.

The pursuit party crossed through what is now Bracken County to a point below the present town of Augusta, Kentucky, and followed the shore of the Ohio River to a point opposite the Little Miami River. There they found the Natives had crossed on a raft, so the party also made a raft, crossed with their horses and explored the valley of the Little Miami up to Old Town, which is present-day Xenia. Realizing how greatly they were outnumbered and the low probability of success, the pursuit was abandoned. Having seen the beautiful land on their journey, Stites wanted to explore more and convinced the rest of the group to return via the Great Miami Valley area of Mill Creek. While the settlers were greatly disappointed of the failed expedition to return their horses, Stites was excited and told the group that he had found something far better than horses: the fertile land between the Little and Great Miami Rivers. In addition to rich soil ideal for farming, there was

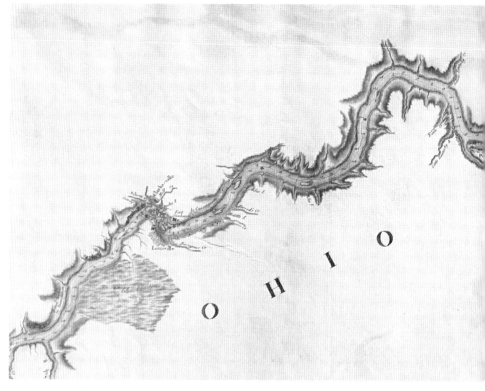

A General Map of the River Ohio Plate the Third shows the Ohio River and first white settlements. *Cincinnati History Library and Archives.*

quality clay, stone, a wide variety of trees for food and construction, many animals to hunt (including deer, bear and wild turkey) and access to major rivers for transportation and trading.

Stites was so impressed by the natural advantages of the region, which he had explored by accident, that he quickly decided to return and make permanent settlement in the Miami Country. He closed his trading venture in Washington, Kentucky, returned to his family in Pennsylvania and quickly journeyed to Trenton, New Jersey, where he tried to convince Congress to sell him land. His first request was not granted, so he appealed directly to John Cleves Symmes, a congressman from Trenton, New Jersey, who went to see the land himself. Upon returning, Symmes purchased 1 million acres of land at sixty-six cents per acre, one of the two first major purchases of land in the Northwest Territory. Symmes sold Stites 20,000 acres along the Little Miami River, including

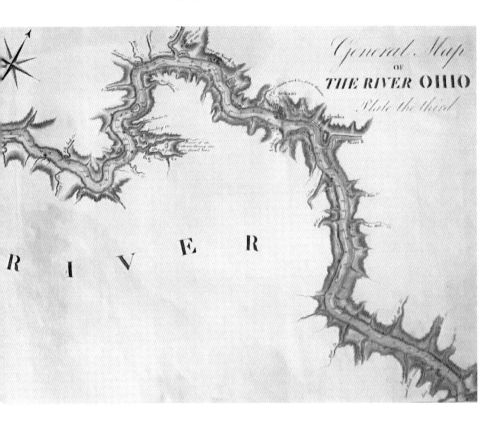

the part at the junction with the Ohio River and a part near Mill Creek, as a reward for bringing the land to his attention.

Stites quickly assembled a settlement group and brought them and his family to Limestone to prepare for settlement. The flatboat journey on the Ohio River was fraught with dangers, from logs smashing into the boats; large, embedded branches in the river that a boat could run into; and sandbars that could ground a boat. The site they chose for settlement was where the Little Miami emptied into the Ohio River. Since rumor had it that five hundred Natives were anticipating their arrival, Benjamin wanted to build a fort quickly. He and his son, Benjamin went to the woods at Limestone and made a large quantity of clapboards, which they put into a boat. They also made doors of boat planks with hangings affixed. During their time of preparations in Kentucky, Benjamin's nephew Hezekiah Stites was killed by Natives in the woods where the men were making their preparations. On November 16, Stites and his party re-embarked to the area of modern-day Bracken County, where they stopped and started again in time to float down to reach the Little Miami at sunrise to have the day before them to labor. At

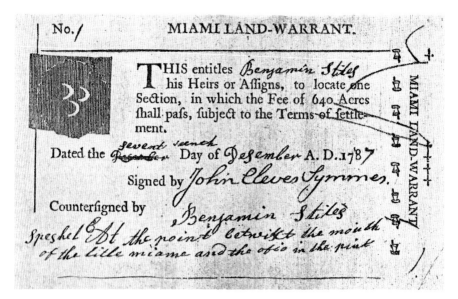

Above: Major Benjamin Stites, leader of the Columbia settlers, acquired twenty thousand acres of the Miami Purchase. *Grace and Truth Church.*

Left: Major Benjamin Stites established Columbia in November 1788. *Dinese Young.*

break of day, the party landed opposite the mouth of the Little Miami and sent five volunteers to look for Natives who might lay in wait. After the signal that all was well, the boats crossed over and landed about three-fourths of a mile below the mouth of the Little Miami, a little after sunrise the morning of November 18, 1788. There were twenty-six settlers in all, including three married women, two girls and two young boys. It was rumored that five-year-old, raven-haired Rachel Stites, daughter of Major Stites, was the first to step out of the boat and onto their new land.

Those present in the first boat load of Columbia settlers were:

Major Benjamin Stites
Mrs. Benjamin Stites
Benjamin Stites Jr.
Rachel Stites
Mr. and Mrs. Greenbright Bailey
James and Reason Bailey
Able Cook
Jacob Mills
Elijah Mills
Ephrain Kibby
John and Mary Gano
Thomas Wade
Elijah Stites
Jonathan Stites
Hezekiah Stites
Elizabeth Stites
Edmund Buxton
Daniel Shoemaker
Daniel Hempstead
Evan Shelby
Allen Woodruff
Hampton Woodruff
Joseph Cox
Benjamin Cox

Immediately upon landing, sentinels were posted, and a clearing was made in a thicket of pawpaws, a native fruit tree, where women and children sat down, with the men standing with guns in hand. A hymn was sung under the leadership of Thomas Wade, and then a prayer of thanksgiving was

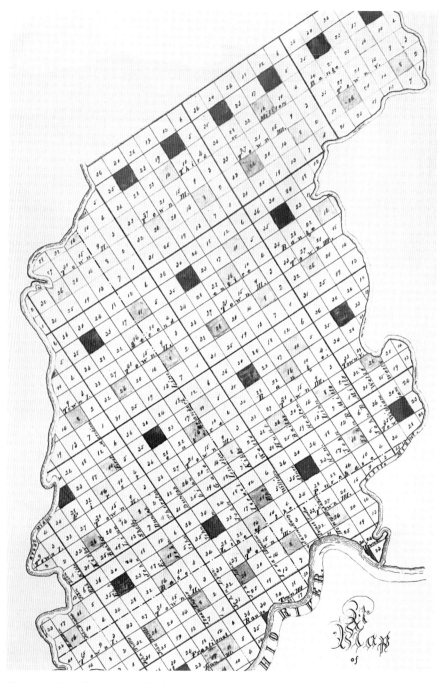

"Symmes Survey" drawn by Charles M. Heaton on September 5, 1824, plotting the entire Symmes Purchase between the Little Miami and Great Miami Rivers. *Cincinnati History Library and Archives.*

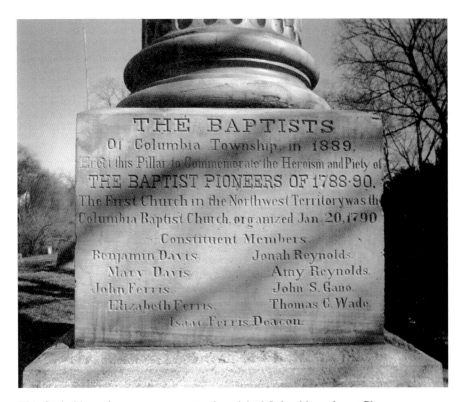

This Corinthian column commemorates the original Columbia settlers at Pioneer Cemetery, *Dinese Young.*

offered. There were multiple Christian religions practiced by the various settlers in the original group. After the close of the service, work was begun on an eighteen-foot-by-twenty-foot blockhouse (on section 29), which was completed about November 24. The original blockhouse stood until it was finally destroyed in 1838.

Oral tradition tells of boats being broken up and used for floors and doors. One of the women supposedly brought with her a looking glass, and the wooden box that had been used to protect it on the journey was set on a barrel and used as a table. Later, it was fitted with handmade rockers and became the community's first crib.

Three additional blockhouses were immediately built by settlers and joined together by palisades, forming a kind of fort termed "Fort Miami." While safety was their primary concern, unbeknownst to them, this provoked attack because to the Natives these blockhouse configurations resembled soldier forts, which represented more permanent claim to the lands and indicators

The village of Columbia at the junction of the Ohio and Little Miami Rivers was the first settlement in the Miami Purchase. It was founded on November 18, 1788. *Grace and Truth Church.*

of warlike aggression. For a short time, the settlement had the protection of regular soldiers (one sergeant and eighteen privates), but they moved downriver to the next settlement, called Losantiville, where Fort Washington was built. Two years later, this community was renamed Cincinnati after the Society of the Cincinnati, whose members were from the Continental army of the Revolutionary War.

Of course, the white American settlers were not the first people to occupy the land on which they established their new community. People from the Shawnee, Miami and Delaware (Lenape) tribes had both permanent communities and actively hunted and traded in the region. The Columbia settlers were initially on good terms with the Natives, who made frequent visits to the blockhouses and Columbia. The Natives were invited to join the settlers for their first Christmas, which was a time of celebration. The unusually warm weather allowed them to feast outdoors. Large tables were placed by the banks of the river, and the primary dish served was savory pot pies, made in two ten-gallon kettles supervised by a Mrs. Dunn from New Jersey.

However, Lieutenant Kingsbury from Fort Washington was invited with his soldiers to join the feast. When soldiers arrived, the Natives went from pleasant and politely engaged to agitated and on high alert due to years of

A Corinthian column was placed at Pioneer Cemetery near modern-day Lunken Airport commemorating the original Columbia Baptist pioneers. *Linda Wedding.*

negative encounters with soldiers. In a memoir, the Honorable Isaac Dunn, son of pioneer Hugh Dunn, said that the Natives thought that the arrival of the soldiers meant they had been lured to the party as a trap to capture them. They were convinced to stay and peacefully dine with everyone, and all parties had an enjoyable feast and visit. However, tensions and warfare between the U.S. government and Native nations in the Northwest Territory, as well as the massive influx of settlers initiated by the Northwest Ordinance, quickly soured relations between settlers and Natives. By 1789, several settlers had been killed or captured, and both groups were engaging in scalping activities as either aggressor or in retaliation. Settlers paid thirty dollars per Native scalp, an enormous sum at the time.

Columbia's initial settlement occurred on the fertile low plains known as Turkey Bottoms, situated on the eastern side of the Symmes Purchase, about one and a half miles above the Little Miami River's mouth. Named for the abundance of wild turkeys and once cultivated by Native Americans for corn, this area was once also Native burial grounds. Covering about 640 acres, Turkey Bottom was a significant clearing. Some smaller plots near Columbia produced ample corn for both Columbia and Losantiville in the first year. Benjamin Randolph, a resident, planted a 1-acre cornfield but had to leave for New Jersey on business. Upon his return in the fall, he was astonished to discover an impressive crop of 963 bushels, thriving throughout the season without any attention.

In the spring following the founding of the settlement, a flood occurred, consuming every house in the settlement except one. Ultimately, the frequent reoccurrence of flooding caused the settlers to relocate to higher ground on the hills.

Erected in 1789, one of the first cabins stood just east of the intersection of Crawfish Run and the road along the river to Losantiville/Cincinnati. Fortified with stout oak doors, robust hinges and sturdy bars supported by timber, the cabin served as a secure stronghold, featuring portholes on all sides for vigilant defense. With only two small windows, each with four panes, the construction reflected the imperative need for protection against Native attacks in Columbia. Despite ongoing conflicts, social life endured. Following the garrison's completion at Fort Washington, officers arranged balls and weekend gatherings, offering entertainment for Columbia settlers. Regular events—including a grand Fourth of July celebration as well as winter riding, visiting and dancing—showcased the resilient social fabric. Amid these festivities, the community did not neglect religious and educational responsibilities.

Originally the Columbia meeting house, Columbia Baptist was started by Dr. Stephen Gano in 1790 and stood where present-day Pioneer Cemetery is located on Airport Road. *Grace and Truth Church.*

On June 20, 1790, Columbia Baptist Church was established with nine individuals: Benjamin Davis, Mary Davis, John Ferris, Elizabeth Ferris, Jonah Reynolds, Amy Reynolds, John S. Gano, Thomas C. Wade and Deacon Isaac Ferris. The initial church, named the Columbia Meeting House, was built on the current Pioneer Cemetery grounds, becoming the foundation for the Miami Baptist Association. This association's churches expanded across the entire Miami Purchase region. The inaugural school in Columbia emerged on June 21, 1790, initiated by John Reilly,

Above: The first church in the
Northwest Territory was founded
in Benjamin Davis's log cabin at
Columbia on January 20, 1790. *Grace
and Truth Church.*

Right: John Gano was one of nine
original founding members of
the Baptist Church of Columbia.
He ordained Daniel Clark at the
Colombia Church on September 23.
Grace and Truth Church.

a Revolutionary War veteran. His English school, based on a six-month subscription, involved instructors rotating among families. Reilly later held significant roles, such as deputy clerk of the county court and clerk of the territorial legislature. Francis Dunlevy joined in the subsequent year, introducing a classical department. Notably, other settlers in Columbia, beyond the original twenty-one boys and men, achieved prominence in the early days of the settlements.

In 1788, General Arthur St. Clair was made governor of the Northwest Territory. One of his first duties upon arrival in Losantiville in January 1790 was to appoint officers of the militia. The local company of about seventy men was commanded by Captain John S. Gano, one of the original settlers, and was soon employed on relief expeditions to beleaguered stations on the Great and Little Miami Rivers.

Benjamin Stites had ambitious plans to make Columbia a bustling metropolis one day and set about surveying a proposed city as soon as was feasible after landing. It was to occupy the plain between Crawfish Creek and the mouth of the Little Miami—a three-mile-square swath of land. The area was only a mile by three quarters near the Ohio River. This tract of land was platted in blocks of eight lots, each half an acre, and the rest inlets of four and five acres each; 945 inlets are said to have been staked off by surveyors, and streets were laid out at right angles. By the end of 1790, there were fifty cabins, a mill, a church and a school in the Columbia settlement. The Ohio River served this area, like many other river communities, as a primary artery for trade. However, as soon as General Wayne defeated the Natives in the fall of 1794 and the Treaty of Greenville was signed in 1795, the safety of settlers was more ensured, and people began to leave Columbia, therefore slowing its growth, diminishing Stites's vision of a thriving metropolis.

EARLY SETTLEMENT YEARS

There were three original settlements under the Symmes Purchase. On November 18, 1788, Columbia was settled by 26 people. In 1788, Losantiville, which was later renamed Cincinnati, was settled by 12 to 15 people, and when annexed to Cincinnati in 1875, Columbia became Cincinnati's oldest neighborhood with a population of 2,500.

In 1789, North Bend was started with plans for an expansive city to be called Summer, but they were abandoned. The three settlements had a competitive rivalry, and each wanted to be the main business center of the settled region. Columbia was the main contender, but Cincinnati had the soldiers' fort and courts for the area. The fort was originally intended for North Bend, but Major Doughty, who arrived with troops from Fort Harmar with instructions to establish the fort, fell in love with a settler's wife in North Bend—she moved with her husband to Cincinnati. Doughty wanted to follow her, so he abandoned North Bend and instead built Fort Washington in Cincinnati.

The Columbia settlers had at first built on a low plain, whose rich soil made it an ideal location for cultivating corn. Throughout the early settlement years, they supplied the needs of both the settlements of Columbia and Losantiville. The first mill that ground the corn had an unusual method of deriving power. Two flatboats were anchored side by side with a large paddle wheel fastened in between. The Little Miami's current turned the wheel, which operated the millstones.

The monument at Pioneer Cemetery has the names of Columbia's original settlers, with an inscription "To the First Boat Load." *Linda Wedding*

Religion was not neglected during the early days of the Columbia settlement. In the first group were several Baptist families, who gathered for worship services in the blockhouse in 1789. On January 20, 1790, the Columbia Baptist Church, the first Protestant congregation in the Northwest Territory, was organized.

The first pastor was Reverend John Smith of Pennsylvania, who, in addition to his ministerial duties, owned a store and small farm. Smith went on to become one of the first senators to represent Ohio in the U.S. Senate. His friendship with Aaron Burr led to his being charged with treason and his ultimate resignation from the Senate.

By the end of 1790, there were fifty cabins, a mill and a school in the settlement. The Ohio River served this area, like many other river communities, as a primary artery for trade. The Treaty of Greenville was signed in 1795, and the Native Americans were forced to moved west and give up their lands. Without the fear of attack and with government protections after Ohio become a state in 1803, Columbia and Cincinnati

Names of members of the
COLUMBIA CHURCH,
Organized 1790.

1790

Benjamin	Davis
Mary	Davis
Issac	Ferris
Jonah	Reynolds
Amy	Reynolds
Elizabeth	Ferris
John	Ferris
John S.	Gano
Thomas C.	Wade
Elijah	Stites
Rhoda	Stites
Sarah	Stites
Benjamin	Stites
Captain	White
Hezekiah	Stites
Mrs	Ferris
Miss	Ferris
A. O.	Spencer
Mrs.	Garrison
M.	Hanne
Sister	Griffen
Sister	Davis
Rachel	Jarvet
David	Davis
Mrs.	Meeks
Mr.	Smith
Mr.	Baily

1791

Mr.	Clark
Mrs.	Clark
Wm.	Gerard
Mrs. Wm.	Gerard
Ross	Crosley
Mrs. Ross	Crosley
Mr.	Turner
Mrs.	Turner
Joseph	Martin
Mrs. Wm.	Night
Mr.	Muchlehaney
Ruth	Terry
David	Jennings
John	Beal
Sister	Bert
Rosannah	Cox
Catherine	Cook
Sister	Hinkel

1792

Francis	Griffin
Mrs. F.	Griffin
Henry	Tucker
Mary	Tucker
John	Brasley
Rachel	Brasley
Louis	Covalt

1793

Francis	Dunlevy
John Hannah	Heaton
David	Price
Sussannah	Price
Jacob	Frazee
Elizabeth	Frazee
Jonathan	Gerard
Wm.	Night
Sarah	Covolt
Joseph	Frazee
Martha	Frazee
Mary	Stewart
Mary	Baily
Sarah	Ball - 1794

1794

Hannah	Crossley
Benjamin	Archer
Thomas	Sincey
Anna	Archer
Robert	Gobel
Wm.	Digby
Abram	Garrison
John	Decoursey
Joseph	Kelley
Hezekiah Mrs. Keziah	Kelley

1795

Levi	Jennings
John	McIntush
Rev. P.	Smith
Catherine	Smith

1796

Sister	Eaton
Thomas	Shields
Richard	Ayres
Mary	Ayres
Dinah	Ayres
Enos	Randolph
Sarah	Lewens

1797

Abraham	Blue
Elizabeth	Blue
Thomas	Frame
Charlotte	Walker

1798

David	Snodgrass
Hugh	McColm

1799

Priscila	Feam
Hannah	Casto
Rebecca	Wells
Mary	Ferris

1800

Mr.	Maggier
Wm.	Casto

1801

Jessee	Vandalah
Milicent	Foster
Robert	Flack
Ezra	Ferris
Villie Sally	German
Hezekiah	Stites
Isaac	Ferris
Abram	Ferris
Elizabeth	Stites
Caleb	German
Joseph	Crossley
Susannah	Ferris
Catherin	Thomill
Ira	Smith
Elizabeth	Smith
James	Casto
Henry	Jennings
Mary	Clark
Salley	Wade
Thomas	Townsend
Wm.	Crossley
Sally	German
Elsie	Ferris
Isaac	Ferris
John	Wolverton
Hannah	Ferris
Rebecca	Congleton
Abram	Riddly
David	Jennings
Joseph	Billings
Patience	Riddley
Jotty	Congleton
Richard	Shaw
Joseph	Congleton
Elizabeth	Shaw
John	Ferris
James	Lyon
Manasses	Braan
Nathan	Shaw
Dally	Jennings
Joseph	Clark
Steven	Flinn
Phoebe	Shaw
Polly	Right
Rebecca	Marsh

Seen here are names of earliest Columbia Baptist Church members. *Grace and Truth Church.*

prospered. New people arrived by flatboat every day. With the advent of the steamboat, the Ohio River became one of the most important avenues of transportation and commerce, and Cincinnati became an important port. In 1791, Columbia became part of Columbia Township. From the early 1840s, it was then included in Spencer Township.

Columbia originally had more people and flourished more than any of the other settlements in the Symmes purchase for the first two to three years, but that did not last. As early as 1794, proprietors gave up on the idea of a prolific town due to the floods. Additionally, Benjamin Stites's untimely death in August 1804, followed closely on October 23 by that of William Brown, a strong leader in the community, left the village without the stewardship for continued growth. Cincinnati benefited from this decline of Columbia, whose remaining leaders moved downriver to the prosperous trading and shipping center.

By 1807, Columbia boasted 250 inhabitants and featured sixty blocks with half-acre lots totaling 945 available lots. Notably, a section on the hillside, initially named Morristown after settler John Morris, flourished under his influence. To evade frequent flooding issues, Columbia relocated in 1815 from Turkey Bottom to the base of Tusculum Hill (now Alms Park), encompassing Morristown. Despite the advent of the Little Miami Railroad connecting it to Cincinnati, the settlement experienced gradual growth. Hindered by persistent flooding, Columbia never attained the envisioned status as a major commercial hub. It obtained village incorporation in 1868, electing J.L. Thompson as the inaugural mayor, with the population then reaching 2,500 residents.

Compared to the settlement years, life in Columbia was somewhat prosperous. Residents made it clear that their community was no place for a freeloader to visit. Early histories of the area talk of boarding paupers at farmhouses. The person would be put up for auction and would go to the lowest bidder. Other documents forbade certain families who were known indigents from entering the town. The houses built in the early nineteenth century reflect a greater sense of prosperity and a lessened need to merely provide a method of survival.

The last of the original settlement blockhouses was destroyed on April 26, 1838, during a seasonal flood. Coincidentally, the same day when the steamboat *Moselle*'s engine exploded killing 150 out of 250 passengers, two passing steamboats near Columbia created a very high wake, causing the already elevated river levels to flood the embankment, where the aged and decrepit blockhouse barely stood erect. The wake washed out the remains

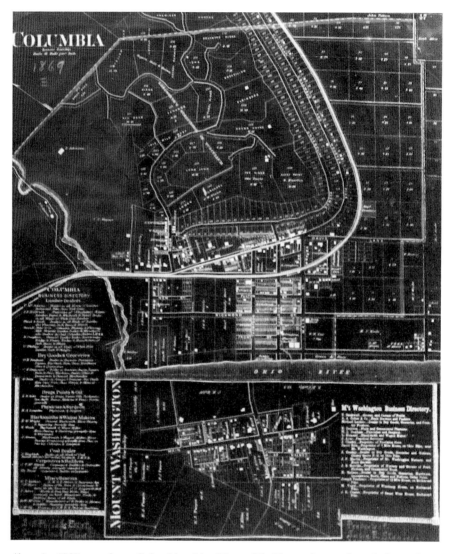

Above: An 1869 map shows Columbia with a Mount Washington insert. *Carnegie Center of Columbia Tusculum.*

Opposite, top: The oldest continuously occupied home in Hamilton County stands at 3644 Eastern Avenue and is referred to as Morris House. *Dinese Young*

Opposite, bottom: Steamboats from early 1800s on the Ohio River. *Clara Hoffmeister.*

of the last original settlement house downriver to an audience of Columbia residents who had gathered to watch the steamers.

Beginning in 1795, Martin Baum, known as the Father of German Immigration to Cincinnati, recruited many early Germans to Cincinnati. Columbia was one of many neighborhoods that witnessed an influx of German immigrants, especially in the 1830s, when there was a boom in meatpacking and shipping in Cincinnati. Additionally, the raging success of Nicholas Longworth's Catawba wine production from Longworth Vineyards attracted an abundance of German immigrant workers.

Opposite: German-born Columbia resident Conrad Kemmeter (1830–1917). *Vickie Rafferty.*

Right: In the early to mid-1800s, the first St. Stephen sign in Columbia bore a German inscription, highlighting its roots. *Dinese Young.*

At the beginning of the 1930s, it was estimated that 5 percent of people living in Cincinnati were of German descent, but within ten years it had increased by 10 percent. Cincinnati, Milwaukee and St. Louis were referred to as the German Triangle due to the massive immigration of Germans to the three areas due to the political and religious oppression during that time in Germany. Many of the immigrants in Cincinnati came from Northern Germany. There were so many Germans in Columbia that they started St. Stephen Catholic Church, which conducted Sunday mass in German.

After a separate existence and slight rivalry with Losantiville, which became Cincinnati, Columbia officially incorporated in 1868 and ultimately merged with Cincinnati in 1873, making Columbia the oldest neighborhood in Cincinnati.

VICTORIAN BOOM

The transportation boom of the late 1800s caused many changes in Columbia. The town developed in population and commerce and was officially incorporated in 1868. As the growth continued and access to the city became more convenient, in 1873, Columbia was annexed by the City of Cincinnati. In 1872, Columbia had 3,184 residents, but by the 1880 census, its population had boomed to 5,358. The concept of suburban life where those with disposable income could escape the growing stench and filth of downtown living was growing in appeal, especially when transportation growth kept outlying communities connected.

   With the influx of people, there was also a housing boom, which is why the community to this day is known for its Victorian architecture. The combination of increased economic affluence due to the Industrial Revolution, the greater access to skilled craftsmen and the elaborate aesthetic of the Victorian era produced buildings with ornate details, quality building materials, intricate "gingerbread" trim, vibrant colors and artistic accents. Vibrant paint colors were popular, and people who could afford to often used polychromatic exteriors to accentuate the house's intricate detailing. This concept was amplified in the mid-1900s across America as interest in restoring and preserving Victorian architecture became popular and owners got very creative with their flamboyant exterior color combinations. Houses with these intensified color combinations were dubbed "Painted Ladies," and the term is still used today. This signature look is what Columbia Tusculum is still famously known for in modern times, and residents enjoy preserving the look of this era.

Most of the buildings seen today were begun in conjunction with the development of transportation in this area. The ease of access to Cincinnati and other communities, as well as the ability to escape the filth and smell of downtown Cincinnati, encouraged people to build their luxurious homes here. Many large agricultural estates were subdivided and sold for building lots in the late 1800s.

This connectivity also enhanced social life in the community. Prominent residents Charles and Carrie Stites wrote in personal diaries of enjoying performances in Mozart Hall, teas at the St. Nicholas, meetings at Burnet House, plays at Pike's Opera house and buggy rides across the Suspension Bridge. The transportation connected the community for commercial growth as well as social enrichments.

Nicholas Longworth, Cincinnati's inaugural millionaire, amassed extensive landholdings, with his vineyards stretching from today's Eden Park to Alms Park, renowned for his popular Catawba wine nationwide. The area around Tusculum was where the grapes for his most prized wines were grown. However, the combination of black rot and labor loss during the Civil War led to the vineyards' demise. Following Longworth's 1863 death, the land was subdivided into Longworth's Tusculum. In 1890, Columbia Heights emerged on Tusculum Avenue's hill, prized for river views, proximity to Larz Anderson's estates, floodplain avoidance and downtown convenience. Despite expectations, the Columbia area maintained a rural charm, earning the nickname "Nanny Goat Hill" due to its animal residents.

In 1919, grocery tycoon Barney Kroger acquired thirteen and a half acres from the original Vineyard Hills, once part of Longworth's estate, to build a Tudor-style mansion. Kroger, the founder of the nation's largest supermarket chain, pioneered the concept of consolidating various departments under one roof, revolutionizing the consumer shopping experience.

As population grew, the business district along Eastern Avenue also experienced growth in the late 1800s. Many businesses—such as hotels, restaurants and saloons—sprang up to service the passengers and workers from the railroad. However, most businesses were community oriented like drugstores, groceries, hardware stores, photographers and so on.

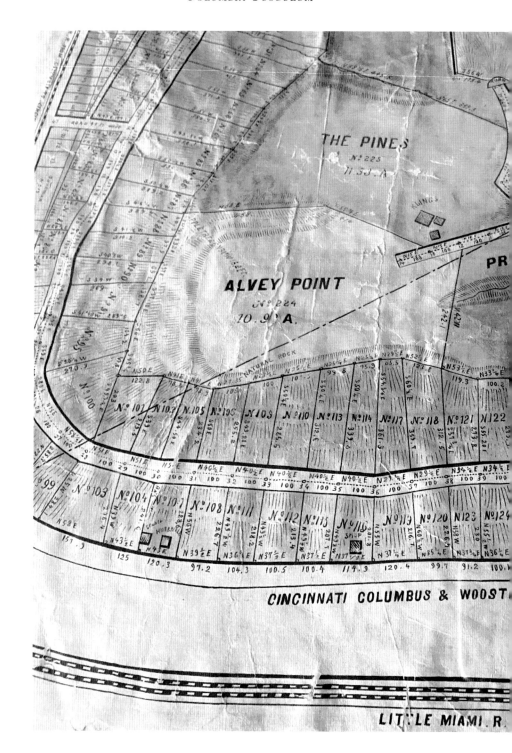

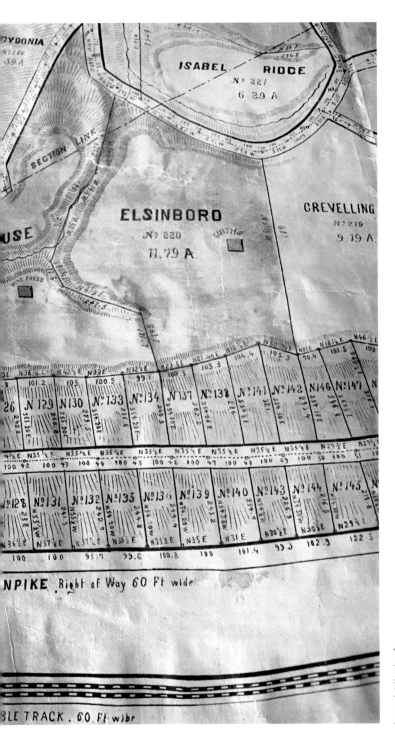

This map shows the Longworth subdivision of Mount Tusculum. *Cincinnati History Library and Archives.*

1913 BUSINESSES IN COLUMBIA TUSCULUM

(not a complete list)

Geo. Quebe
Ladies' and Gents' Up-to-Date Shoes
2458 Eastern Avenue

J.J. Yungbluth & Son Undertakers
2558 Eastern Avenue

Joseph Overberg Furniture Hospital
3229 Eastern Avenue

Richard Wientjes Cafe
3247 Eastern Avenue

Ludlow & Brawley
Grocery and Market
3251–53 Eastern Avenue

H. Schoettmer
Dry Goods Notions
3327 Eastern Avenue

Spaeth & Bauer Groceries and Meats
3704 Eastern Avenue

Nick Schwartz's Barber Shop
3709 Eastern Avenue

Joseph J. Crotty
Plumbing and Gas Fitting
3709 Eastern Avenue

Henry Ketteler Boots and Shoes
3709 Eastern Avenue

The Avenue Confectionery
Tobacco, Cigarettes, Candy, Ice Cream and Soda Water
3731 Eastern Avenue

Walt Flowers
3739 Eastern Avenue

A. Groff Pabst
Millinery, Dry Goods, Gents' Furnishings
3741–43 Eastern Avenue

James A. Shanley Café
3755 Eastern Avenue

Walter Millar
Dry Goods, Notions, Hats, Caps and Clothing
3913–15 Eastern Avenue

W.E. Rust
Notions, Stationery, Toys, Games, Sporting Goods, Candy, Cigars, All
    Cincinnati Papers and Magazines, etc.
3916 Eastern Avenue

W. Tasker & Son Grocers
3938 Eastern Avenue

East End Vulcanizing and Repair Shop
Automobile Repairing
3954 Eastern Avenue

Gus. Wiethron
Wall Paper and Interior Decorations
Window Shades
3960 Eastern Avenue

Karl H. Williams Grocer
4025 Eastern Avenue

Raber Bros. Hardware and Paints
4029 Eastern Avenue

Carrel Lunch Room
4030 Eastern Avenue

The Bennet Hardware Company
Hardware, Seeds, Harness, Shoes, Paints, Glass and Fencing
4744–46 Eastern Avenue

The Eastern Avenue Pharmacy
4909 Eastern Avenue

F.H. Poske
French Dry Cleaning & Tailoring Company
4921 Eastern Avenue

The Seelmeyer & Fox Company
Hay, Grain, Feed and Poultry Supplies
Eastern Avenue and Kemper Lane

Joseph Schneider
Druggist
Eastern and Tusculum Avenues

Linwood Pharmacy
Harry H. Lahke
Linwood and Eastern Avenues

New Delta Cafe
Uhrig & Loebig
Eastern Avenue and Strader Street

Miss Miriam A. Corcoran
Hair Work of All Kinds
3320 Walworth Avenue

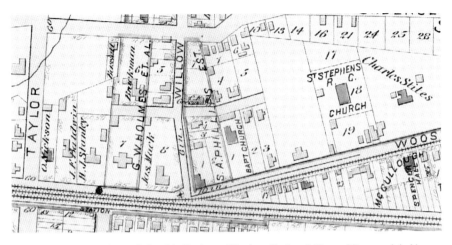

An 1884 Platt map shows Columbia Business District. *Cincinnati History Library and Archives.*

Thos. H. Heatley
Painter
Delta and Linwood Avenues

Schmidt and Rech Groceries
3567 Columbia Avenue

W.M. Buschur
Horse Shoer and General Blacksmith
319 Stanley Avenue

Mr. Witschger
House Raiser and Mover
457 Missouri Avenue

C.W. Moss
Coal, Lime, Cement, Sand Gravel and Sewer Pipe
218 Tennyson Street

Several older residents have been quoted as saying that by the turn of the century, the business district supplied the total needs of the community. The frequent runs of the streetcar and the steam dummy provided easy access to the shopping district for residents outside the immediate area.

This hillside house shows the bridge between rural Columbia and Victorian development. *Brian Williams.*

Queen City Forging on Tennyson Street started in the 1880s making hardware for carriages. *Janette Jackson.*

First- or second-grade teachers and pupils at McKinley School on December 18, 1895, when the school was the Twenty-Fourth District School. *Carnegie Center of Columbia Tusculum.*

The section of Eastern Avenue from Davis Lane (Airport Road) to Delta Avenue boasted at least five groceries, two hotels, three hardware stores, four salons, three barbers, two banks, a theater, four shoe stores, a restaurant, four dry good stores, three confectioners, three drugstores, a jeweler, a plumber and a tailor. In addition to the stores, there were doctors, a lawyer, an architect and several undertakers. A major employer was the Boldt Glass Company on Davis Lane. The police station was located on Eastern Avenue near Tennyson. The paddy wagon and horses were kept at the police patrol at the corner of Columbia and Delta. Unlike businesses today, the shopkeepers lived either above or near their place of business. In 1871, households could pay $0.25 for beef steak, $0.07 for a loaf of bread, $0.10 for a dozen ears of corn, $0.30 for watermelon, $0.40 for four quarts of raspberries, $0.09 for a pound of crackers, $1.80 for ten yards of fabric, $0.70 for a haircut and wash, $1 for a week's laundry wash and $1 for a streetcar ticket. The sense of community and commerce was very strong.

Tusculum's first resident was John Morris, an original settler of Columbia. Morris became one of the largest landowners in the community. Later, another Morris, Thomas Morris, started a store on the hillside to the north

Teachers at McKinley Elementary School. At this time, women were not allowed to teach if they were married. *Carnegie Center of Columbia Tusculum.*

Mrs. Rosa Fry's all-male students at McKinley Elementary. *Carnegie Center of Columbia Tusculum.*

At 259 Carrell Street, a woman and child are on the porch of a Victorian house with intricate gingerbread trim. *Brian Williams.*

of Columbia somewhere on what is now Columbia Parkway. A cluster of houses grew up around it, which gradually crept up the hill once called Bald Hill and became known as Tusculum Hill. Tusculum also expanded southwest to the river, where steamboat building became the major industry. By 1875, Tusculum Avenue had extended from the crest of Tusculum Hill down to Undercliff Avenue (present-day Columbia Parkway), where the section between Undercliff and Eastern Avenues was called Willow Run. In the late eighteenth century, this area was heavily populated by people engaged in the shipbuilding industry.

One thousand acres of land around Bald Hill was deeded by Congress to Major Silas Howell, a hero of the Revolutionary War. A Native American trail running through part of this land eventually became known as Grandin Road. Major Howell's daughter, Susan Howell Connor, married a pioneer by the name of Nicholas Longworth I, who successfully developed the land into prized vineyards. Tusculum Hill was at one time a tangle of grapevines grown by Nicholas Longworth I, maker of the immensely popular Catawba and Golden Wedding wines.

The top of Tusculum Hill became a very fashionable section where mansions and estates of the affluent were built away from the flooding and commercial odors and filth of the river valley villages and downtown Cincinnati. Part of this hilltop was named Tusculum Heights (or "Longworth's Tusculum") and is a part of Alms Park now, managed by Cincinnati Parks Board. The entire area of Tusculum was never incorporated, but it was annexed with the rest of Spenser Township in 1875 and was soon merged into the Columbia community. This explains the neighborhoods' modern name of Columbia Tusculum.

The Victorian era is when some of Columbia Tusculum's most enduring architecture was created. Many homes were occupied by multiple-generation families and by prominent residents.

BATES BUILDING, 3819 EASTERN AVENUE

One of the oldest buildings on Eastern Avenue in the neighborhood, the Bates House was constructed in 1865. The Bates Building is a historic house in the Columbia Tusculum neighborhood. The two-story building was constructed in a functional domestic style of architecture. In 1979, the Bates Building was listed in the National Register of Historic Places. Despite its age, this building is recognized as green because it has one green activity that achieved outcomes required for historic preservation properties to be labeled "green." One long-term resident of the home was Karl Braun, who was born about 1894. He lived in Cincinnati, Ohio, with his wife, Lenora, and their son and six daughters. The home was named after owners Rudolph and Dorothy Bates, who owned the home from 1977 until 2017.

LANDT BUILDING, 3815 EASTERN AVENUE

Located on Eastern Avenue in the Columbia Tusculum historic district, this large, 4,400-square-foot home was originally built as a single-family structure. Built in 1895, it is a unique amalgamation of architectural styles, including Georgian and Victorian, and transitions into much simpler styles from the late 1800s and early 1900s. The front of the home has mirrored symmetry in its dual front entries and rounded bay windows. Inconsistent and varied levels of ornamentation can be found from cornice dentils, bay windows, floor overhangs and basic floor plans. It's named after one-time owner Dorothy Landt, who purchased the property in 1976, and was owned by the American Legion East End Post 358 in the 1940s. In 1979, the home was listed in the National Register of Historic Places.

LANGDON HOUSE, 3624 EASTERN AVENUE

Known as the Langdon House, the frame Gothic Revival home at 3624 Eastern Avenue was built by Dr. Wesley Elstun and purchased in 1865 by Dr. Henry Archer Langdon, a noted Civil War surgeon. When he returned from the war, he held private practice in a small building on the front of this property that complemented the architectural style of the home. The small office building can now be visited at Sharonwoods' Heritage Village Museum. The home displays board-and-batten wall treatment and four arched Gothic bay windows on the veranda. The interior is distinguished by an eighteen-foot domed ceiling on the second floor. It was built in 1855.

STANLEY HOUSE, 3618 EASTERN AVENUE

Constructed in 1865 by General Stanley, a Union officer and city engineer, 3618 Eastern Avenue underwent restoration to reclaim its initial splendor. The project included reinstating the original grandeur with a front porch and veranda replacement. During renovations, previous owners uncovered quoins, rare wooden elements mimicking masonry, on the original siding. In Cincinnati, only a handful of houses feature such distinctive quoins, according to The Carnegie Center of Columbia Tusculum.

MORRIS HOUSE, 3642 EASTERN

Morris House is the oldest continuously inhabited dwelling in Hamilton County. This symmetrical 2.5-story frame vernacular is distinguished by a center gable, five bay windows and a Victorian porch. The original log cabin was built in 1804, and then later modifications came in 1830. (See pages 117 and 118 for more information.)

STEVENS HOUSE, 3718 MORRIS PLACE

Known as the Stevens House (see opposite page), this Stick shingle Victorian home at 3718 Morris was built in 1881 for Columbia Baptist's pastor, Reverend W.E. Stevens. Architect Charles Crapsey, known for designing many prominent churches, designed the home. His signature style infused artistic character and employed creative uses of massing, shapes and materials with varied roof shapes, wall treatments and asymmetrical massing. It incorporated many Victorian architectural features such as curved glass bay windows, carved wood entry ceiling, multi-level floors and more. The home features an exterior ashlar foundation; brick accents; shingle siding; six custom ornate fireplaces, four of which are Eastlake; and mixed maple and oak and pine floors.

3615 MORRIS PLACE

This home was built in 1881 by a grocery store owner named Stegemeyer. One of its most notable features is its square tower. Owners in the late 1980s restored the exterior to its original design based on research.

3631 MORRIS PLACE

The house at 3631 Morris Place is a home that had just two owners for its first eighty-seven years of existence. The home was built in 1907 by Parley and Anna Perrin. Parley was a coal merchant turned electrician. They raised their two children, Rhoda and Chester, in the house. Anna remained at the residence for eleven years after Parley's passing, selling to George and Irma Brofft in 1949. Irma held on to the property until 1994.

Reverend W.E. Stevens served for more than twenty-three years at Columbia Baptist Church and built this house at 3718 Morris Place in 1880. *Ben and Dinese Young.*

3710 Morris Place. *Dinese Young.*

3710 MORRIS PLACE

Constructed between 1868 and 1869, 3710 Morris Place stands as one of the pioneering homes in the Longworth Subdivision of Mount Tusculum. The original lot, leased in February 1868, mandated the erection of a house valued at a minimum of $1,500 within five years. Early maps suggest that R.H. Langdale may have built the home, later transferring it to Henry Faber, an attorney and president of Aurora Mire and Marine Insurance Company, in 1871. Langdale and Faber cofounded Queen City Commercial College in 1874 while residing in Columbia Tusculum. Although both opted not to purchase the leased land, Thomas Longworth Jr. of Madisonville acquired it in 1881, utilizing it for rental purposes until selling it to Anna Perrin. In 1907, Anna and her husband constructed another home at 3631 Morris Place. It was not until the 1920s that the property transitioned to its first long-term owner-occupants.

3732 MORRIS PLACE

Built by I. Stites, this 1887 Victorian home is a combination of Queen Anne and Roman Gothic styles. The interior features six original leaded and stained-glass windows, hardwood flooring and ten-foot ceilings. The deed records indicate that the home was originally built for Martha F. Morris and her sister, Louise J. (Morris) Montfort, both dependents of the pioneer J.C. Morris.

315 TUSCULUM AVENUE

The house at 315 Tusculum was built in 1895 by Dr. Edwin Behymer and his wife, Jennie. Dr. Behymer was one of the best-known physicians in the East End/Columbia area and actively engaged in local politics. The Behymer family lived at this residence until Dr. Behymer died suddenly of heart trouble in 1916.

315 Tusculum Avenue. *Dinese Young.*

317 Tusculum Avenue.
Dinese Young.

317 TUSCULUM AVENUE

The house at 317 Tusculum was built in 1895 by Morris Lien, a wholesale clothing merchant who had lived in Columbia Tusculum since coming from Northern Ireland in 1850 at ten months old. Morris and his wife, Susie, raised their family in this Tusculum Avenue home. When Morris died in 1930, he was considered one of the oldest residents in the community. The house remained in the Lien family until 1973.

322 TUSCULUM AVENUE

Once the home and office of Dr. M.B. Brady of Hamilton County Board of Health, this home was built in 1880. The house retains original woodwork, oak floors, pocket doors and typical stained glass. The older rear section of the house was said to be where Dr. Brady treated community patients in a private practice.

COTTAGE ON TUSCULUM HILL, 516 TUSCULUM AVENUE

Number 516 Tusculum Avenue, known as "Cottage on Tusculum Hill," was a workingmen's cottage in Tusculum Heights subdivision. It was built in 1880.

516 Tusculum Avenue. *Dinese Young.*

FEE HOUSE, 325 TUSCULUM AVENUE

This Queen Anne–style house at 325 Tusculum was built by Harley Broadwell in 1893 for $6,000. Harley and his brother Cyrus were traveling salesmen for paper companies and purchased the sizable lot to build family homes for themselves and their brother Isaac. The boys had lived with their mother in a rental house on Morris Place since her divorce from their father, Ambrose, in 1871. Harley tragically died within days of moving into the newly built house. His young widow, Estelle, became a local socialite, hosting regular meetings and social events in the home. One day, her high school sweetheart reconnected; they married and eventually moved to St. Louis. Afterward, the home was owned by John Edward Breen, a local engineer, followed by Dr. Frank Fee. Dr. Fee was a prominent Cincinnati surgeon and chief of staff at Christ Hospital, and he lived in the home with his wife, Gertrude, from 1907 to 1926. Special features of this home include the corner tower/turret and geometrical pattern leaded glass windows.

STITES HOMESTEAD

The Stites homestead was built in 1800 by Anna Carter, daughter of Benjamin Stites. Benjamin Stites died in this house in 1804. It was located on Davis Lane (now Airport Road) and was razed in 1915.

STITES HOUSE, 315 STITES AVENUE

The Stites House at 315 Stites Avenue is in the National Register of Historic Places. The home was built by Hezekiah Stites Jr., nephew of Benjamin Stites, in 1835 and was expanded by his son, Charles, in 1867. Hezekiah Jr. went by the nickname "Kiah" and was an active river trader and pork packer who took goods down the Ohio River as far as New Orleans. In 1829, he married Ruth Ferris. Hezekiah Jr. bought 2.5 acres from the J.C. Morris estate at auction in 1835 for $710. The brick home with stone foundation was built in the Federal and Greek Revival styles, with a distinctly Victorian porch on the 1867 addition. The original front portion of the house had only four rooms and featured a large entrance hall, eighteen-inch-thick brick walls, a circular staircase and first- and second-floor rear porches and had many wooden pegs used in its construction in place of nails. The house featured marble mantels in the living room and master bedroom and a six-foot-long wooden mantel over the large kitchen open-hearth fireplace.

Ruth gave birth to six children, only two of whom survived until adulthood, and passed away at the age of twenty-six. Kiah married her older sister, Mary. Ruth's daughter Mollie was such a beauty that she was known the "Belle of Tusculum" and had many suitors. She married Penn Nixon, editor of Chicago's *Inter Ocean*, but unfortunately passed away six months afterward. Kiah's remaining sole heir, Charles, married his cousin Carrie Stites and lived in the house. Charles managed an iron measure factory until it burned, and the family were forced to economize and build another home in Mariemont.

For a time, the house was a boardinghouse for employees of the Charles Boldt Glass Company on Carrell Street. In 1905, it was converted into apartments.

1900s

Columbia experienced enormous evolution through the 1900s. Life in the early, prosperous 1900s community differed significantly from the mid-1900s, when urban blight and economic changes brought about decline in economy and infrastructure. The socioeconomic landscape of the community changed significantly compared to the previous one hundred years and continued to evolve over the next one hundred years. The immigrant, blue-collar working-class residents of the early twentieth century significantly differed from the gentrification and young professional, white-collar residents at the start of the twenty-first century. Once again, interest in convenient urban, walkable communities fueled a new housing boom where vacant lots and ramshackle homes were sites for new, large urban homes by the dozens.

Described as tightly knit, the community in the early 1900s boasted numerous affluent residents who actively looked out for the less fortunate. With everyone residing and working in the area, a robust sense of pride permeated the community. The convenience of a walkable community with homes close to one another helped neighbors get to know one another. Local law enforcement, living among the residents, knew everyone personally. During nightly patrols, policemen meticulously inspected every property, tapping their sticks on porches to signal their presence. Horse-drawn wagons handled most deliveries, including home-delivered ice until around 1920, and cobblestone paving facilitated the challenging terrain of steep hillside streets. Streetcars and railways provided transportation outside of the community and made the community well connected in Cincinnati.

The construction of East End Library was funded by Andrew Carnegie Foundation in 1906. The library served the community until 1959.

Saloon in the Columbia business district in the early 1900s. *Brian Williams.*

McKinley Elementary students from the early 1900s. *Carnegie Center of Columbia Tusculum.*

It was known to be a tight-knit community where residents grew up, stayed in the neighborhood and expanded their small businesses. Landsdorf Hardware was one of the oldest in Cincinnati and was operated by two sisters, Elizabeth and Catherine Langsdorf. Another female resident, Mabel Overshiner, lived in the community her entire life and operated Heatley Hardware at 3801 Eastern Avenue. Showing progressive changes, several homes listed women as single owners on deeds.

In the early 1900s, the prevalent mode of transportation for community residents was horse-drawn. Some individuals possessed their own horses and carriages, while others would rent them when necessary. Undertakers often maintained stables to house numerous horses. Concurrently, streetcars and railroads remained integral, ensuring the community's vibrancy and accessibility. As time progressed, the community underwent a shift toward automobiles with the rest of the nation, transforming into a hub for car transportation when Columbia Avenue was converted into a higher-speed parkway in the 1940s.

The community's women were renowned for organizing social events, including parades benefiting various causes. During World War I, a notable event organized by local women involved a week-long festival with a circus tent, featuring locals dressed as "wild animals" and culminating in a chariot race and parade. Likewise, groups like the Red Cross gathered at the East End Library, now known as the Carnegie Center of Columbia Tusculum, to wrap and package bandages for the war effort. Civic organizations such as the Masons at Yeatman's Lodge became very popular in this period.

A grocery store on Eastern Avenue. *Janette Jackson.*

A group of Columbia residents posing with a Model T automobile. *Ben and Dinese Young. Carnegie Center of Columbia Tusculum.*

Red Cross volunteers during World War I at East End Library. *Carnegie Center of Columbia Tusculum.*

Young people's leisure activities included music lessons, East End branch library visits and winter sledding down Tusculum Hill. The east wing of the library was the children's section and had a stage for puppet shows and other children's performances. The Carrel Street Railroad Station and the YMCA served as popular gathering spots for boys, with the latter organizing sports teams and community activities.

Despite the Ohio River being a vital transportation route, it posed its share of challenges for the community, mostly relating to its proclivity to flooding. For example, during the winter of 1904–5, there was such a deep freeze that the Ohio River was impassable for fifty-six days. The river was not only frozen all the way to the river bottom, but ice was also piled up as high as thirty feet. Steamers were wrecked, all rail traffic stopped and there were coal shortages due to the destruction of coal barges and the impassibility of the river.

History repeated itself in the disastrous ice gorge and flood of 1918. On December 8, 1917, Cincinnati experienced a snowstorm with a record of eleven inches of snow. In addition to this shutting the city's transportation down, the Ohio River froze shore to shore around January 1, 1918. On New Year's Day 1918, Cincinnatians ice skated across the Ohio River in

The Young Men's Christian Association (YMCA) at the corner of Columbia and Delta Avenues. *Janette Jackson.*

A horse and buggy on Eastern Avenue in front of East End Library. *Carnegie Center of Columbia Tusculum.*

celebration of the holiday. Through January, the situation became dire, as six more inches fell—unmanned barges and boats were torn loose, and large chunks of ice crashed into and sank other barges and boats.

On January 30, enough melting occurred that a large crack was heard as ice began splitting. The melting tributaries caused giant ice slabs to rush into the Ohio River, causing a twenty-foot swell of ice and water to hit downtown Cincinnati on February 1, causing the river to rise sixty-one feet. Boats and barges that had been stuck in the ice crashed and sank. In addition to more than one hundred coal barges sinking, coal yards along the river flooded. The shortage of coal almost shut down the power plant that supplied heat and light to the city.

While other floods, like those in 1913 and 1924, also affected Columbia, the most significant flood was the Great Flood of 1937. This devastating flood, with a crest of eighty feet, is referred to as the "Greatest Natural Disaster in Tristate History," as it left 1 million people homeless and caused an estimated 350 deaths. The Ohio flooded from Pittsburgh to Illinois. It's estimated that 15 to 20 percent of Cincinnati was covered in water, and the river's crest surpassed the previous record height by almost nine feet. Much of the rain causing the flooding took place over twelve days in mid-January.

In Columbia, the waters of the river inundated Stanley Avenue, Eastern Avenue and most streets leading up to the parkway. In response, residents

A street in Columbia showing the effects of the 1918 winter flood and ice gorge. *Ben and Dinese Young.*

The flooding often went up to East End Library on Eastern Avenue. Here a rowboat is used by residents to navigate the streets. *Carnegie Center of Columbia Tusculum.*

ingeniously navigated boats through the flooded streets, aiding their neighbors and evacuating their homes. The flooding resulted in extensive damage, yet the community's resilient spirit, exemplified by the "Y Marines," played a pivotal role in the rescue operations.

The Great Depression added to the challenge, straining federal, state and local resources. The widespread destruction, coupled with the economic hardships of the era and intensified by the timing of the event, led to a loss of property, community damage and psychological trauma. These factors collectively contributed to the economic suppression experienced by the river town community in the mid-1900s.

Following World War II, significant transformations swept through the community as returning veterans sought new and affordable housing in the suburbs. Concurrently, a substantial migration of Appalachians unfolded from the Appalachian Highlands, spanning eastern Kentucky, West Virginia and parts of Alabama, Georgia, Kentucky, Maryland, Mississippi, North Carolina, Ohio, Pennsylvania, South Carolina, Tennessee and Virginia. This migration was facilitated by the availability of homes left vacant during the suburban exodus. During this time, the community became referred to as East End and encompassed the communities of Linwood, Columbia and what was once known as Fulton.

Kellogg Bridge over the Little Miami River. It is looking toward the East End from a nearby hill during the great flood of 1937. *Brian Williams.*

Upon their arrival in Cincinnati in the 1940s, Appalachians were initially referred to as "mountaineers" or "mountain people." Faced with the nationwide decline in the coal mining industry, a substantial number of Appalachian individuals sought improved economic opportunities and a higher quality of life by migrating to industrialized cities like Detroit, Chicago, Cleveland, Cincinnati, Pittsburgh, Baltimore, Washington, D.C., Milwaukee, Toledo and Muncie, Indiana, extending into the 1970s.

Southern Ohio's industrial towns, including Dayton and Cincinnati, were particularly favored by migrants from eastern Kentucky due to their proximity to their homeland. In Cincinnati, some Appalachian migrants settled in urban neighborhoods, attracted by the availability of factory jobs and industrial opportunities. Other neighborhoods, such as Columbia, appealed to these migrants due to their proximity to downtown, river culture and the abundance of large, empty and affordable homes left behind during the postwar suburban flight.

In response to these demographic shifts, Cincinnati's Urban Appalachian Community Coalition and the Appalachian Festival were established in Cincinnati during the 1970s. These organizations aimed to celebrate the heritage of the Appalachian community and preserve its unique culture.

During the late 1970s and 1980s, a resurgence of interest in Victorian architecture and rising gas prices for commuters contributed to a migration back to the city core, sparking community restoration initiatives

Above: In 1907, CG&P's terminus was at Carrel and Dumont Streets. *Mark Beatty.*

Right: A pedestrian shopping on Eastern Avenue near East Side Grill. *Brian Williams.*

and a renewed sense of pride. Simultaneously, there was a revival of the communal spirit reminiscent of the neighborhood's early days, with residents actively engaging in architectural restoration, community council projects and the redevelopment of both the historic business district on Eastern Avenue and the creation of "Columbia Square," an urban design plan for a new business district on Columbia Parkway.

In 1979, seventeen Columbia Tusculum properties were part of a collective submission for a historic preservation survey for placement in the National Register of Historic Places. While most of the properties were buildings, the submission also encompassed the Columbia Baptist and Fulton-Presbyterian Cemeteries. Additionally, Columbia Tusculum was named a Cincinnati City Historic District in 1989 and listed in the National Register. The National Register of Historic Places is the official list of the nation's historic places worthy of preservation and was created by the National Historic Preservation Act of 1966. It is managed by the National Park Service to identify and protect America's archaeological resources and sets forth conservation guidelines and restriction for historic building rehabilitation, alterations and improvements. The Columbia Tusculum Historic District's borders are Eastern Avenue between Tusculum Avenue and Stites Avenue, all of Morris

Kris Lemmon uncovered and then replicated the original paint colors and stenciling in the East End Library during renovations to the Carnegie Center of Columbia Tusculum. *Carnegie Center of Columbia Tusculum.*

Place, Donham Avenue, Sachem Avenue, Stevens Place and Creighton Place, as well as Tusculum Avenue from Eastern Avenue to Alms Park.

Throughout the 1980s and 1990s, extensive restoration and community rebuilding efforts unfolded, leading to the establishment of three community nonprofits: the Columbia Tusculum Community Council, Columbia Tusculum Economic Development Corporation (EDC) and the Carnegie Center of Columbia Tusculum, a nonprofit community center. The EDC was formed to conceive and implement multi-phase Urban Design Plans for Columbia Tusculum's economic redevelopment. Its founding members were Don Fatica, Michael Kovasckitz, J.R. Hirshberg and Dave Vorbeck. Although it achieved success with the development of Columbia Square businesses around the turn of the twenty-first century, the organization eventually disbanded, making way for the Three East Business Association. Key figures in the modern revitalization of Columbia Tusculum included residents like John Van Volkenburgh, Greg Dale, Mike Kovasckitz, Dilip Tripathy, Lois Broerman, Cindy Schrader, Brenda Lugar and Catherine Herring, among many others. In 1994, the abandoned East End Library was purchased by the community, renovated and turned into a nonprofit community arts and culture center still active at the time of publication.

Columbia Tusculum community volunteers, board members and donors in 1997. They established the nonprofit Carnegie Center of Columbia Tusculum community center by restoring the original East End library. *Carnegie Center of Columbia Tusculum.*

A modern mural on Columbia Parkway represents the community's Victorian connection. *Dinese Young.*

While the revitalization efforts and the growing interest in urban residency and lifestyle in the early 2000s made Columbia Tusculum a socioeconomically diverse neighborhood, they also brought about gentrification due to the escalating costs of housing and living, gradually displacing much of the remaining generation of lower-income Appalachian settlers from the mid-1900s. The first quarter of the twenty-first century witnessed an influx of new, high-end homes, shops and urban conveniences, yet Columbia has preserved its community essence as a constantly progressing and evolving community that has linked people and progress in Cincinnati throughout time.

TRANSPORTATION

Transportation has played a central role in the development of Columbia from the start. Columbia was the gateway to Fort Washington, Cincinnati and the rest of Hamilton County, and being situated between the Ohio and Little Miami Rivers, the area evolved into a primary transportation corridor. In addition, the Ohio River connected southwest Ohio to eastern states as well as the Mississippi River and Gulf of Mexico, assisting the movement of people and goods over great distances. Every form of transportation has been active in the community and has been central to its history, growth and continued relevance: flatboats, steamboats, trading routes, railroads, streetcars, parkways, airplanes and more.

The Ohio River has defined and shaped the culture, heritage, development and resources for humans over thousands of years. Its role in transportation and development cannot be underestimated. From the moment Anglo-American settlers arrived on flatboats to modern-day barges transporting bulk forms of raw energy and industrial commodities, riverboats have been a constant presence and integral component of the Columbia community.

Riverboats changed the way people traveled on the Ohio River by increasing speed and passenger capacity exponentially. The first riverboat was launched in 1811 in Pittsburgh and traveled to New Orleans. Cincinnati was quick to seize the development opportunity, launching twenty-five newly built steamboats between 1811 and 1825. With its convenient location on the Ohio River, Cincinnati became one of the most important cities of commerce prior to the Civil War thanks in large part to its shipping industry. In addition to industry, steamboats provided

Passengers disembarking from the *Island Queen* at Coney Island. *Brian Williams.*

transportation for people in business and re-creation. In Columbia and surrounding neighborhoods, the *Island Queen* steamboat would transport passengers to Coney Island for a day of fun.

Fulton, or "Eastern Liberties," home of the Cincinnati Marine Railway and Eureka Dry Dock Company Yard, was established in 1826 and grew to become the center of the most extensive shipbuilding center on the Ohio River. The first shipbuilding yards in the Cincinnati area started in Fulton, which became world famous for its ships. It only took Eastern Liberties four years from the opening of its first shipbuilding yard to grow to a population of 1,089 residents. The village was named for Robert Fulton, an inventor of the steamboat, and it was annexed to Cincinnati in 1854.

In 1852, the Ohio Cincinnati Marine Railway and the Eureka Dry Dock Company yards emerged. Hundreds of steamboats were built there for the Ohio and Mississippi Rivers and for foreign countries as well. *Natchez* was the most famous of those ships, which lost in a famous race with the *Robert E. Lee* steamboat between New Orleans and St. Louis in 1870.

Farther east was the public landing with a fleet of Cincinnati River cruisers at the foot of Strader Avenue, where modern-day Ohio River Yacht Club resides. In its prime, the Ohio River Yacht Club was such a hangout for many politicians, like Garry Herrmann and Rod Hynicka, that it was said more laws were written there than at city hall.

Cincinnati Gymnasium Boat Club on the Ohio River. *Brian Williams.*

By 1910, steamboat traffic on the Ohio River was being replaced by the railroad as a means of transportation. Those boats already on the river continued to operate, but when they became too old for service, they were not replaced. The Ohio continued its periodic rampages—with major floods in 1913, 1918 and 1924—but the most spectacular river disaster was the "ice gorge" of 1918. The Ohio froze over in January, and as late as March it was still possible to walk across the river. Steamboats were imprisoned in the ice, and with the thaw, they were crushed by the shifting ice. After that, the steamboat became more a memory than a mode of transportation.

In 1836, the Little Miami Railroad was incorporated, and by 1841, it was connecting Cincinnati, Columbia and the village of Milford. In 1870, it was absorbed by the Pennsylvania Railroad. In 1917, the tracks were elevated to allow for more speed and safety. Until 1970, the line was among the busiest in Ohio; all passenger traffic to and from Cincinnati on the Pennsylvania passed through Columbia. In 1877, the narrow-gauge Cincinnati, Georgetown and Portsmouth steam railroad inaugurated service between downtown Cincinnati and Clermont County. Around 1917, the steam engines were replaced by electric trains.

Pendleton grew when the Little Miami Railroad opened to traffic in 1843 and the Pennsylvania Railroad shop and roundhouse were built, making Pendleton a thriving railroad village. Pendleton was never incorporated but

In 1922, Hickey's Locomotive no. 21 was a local train. *Brian Williams.*

A steam train powered through Columbia. *Brian Williams.*

Pendleton Railroad Yards was an important switch station. *Vickie Rafferty.*

was annexed to Cincinnati in 1870. The Pendleton Rail Yard was a busy hub for Pennsylvania Railroad cars and was at the base of Walworth Avenue. There were shops and a roundhouse to repair railcars, and it was said that they cleaned engines with benzene, a chemical that has tainted the soil and prohibited growth of flora since. It was abandoned in the 1970s.

On the corner of Carrel Street and Dumont is a monument to what was once the Carrel Street Station. This station was the terminal, yards and maintenance facilities for the Cincinnati Portsmouth and Georgetown Railroad. The Cincinnati, Portsmouth and Georgetown Railroad (CG&P) was a narrow-gauge steam railroad that began in 1876 as Cincinnati and Portsmouth Railroad and functioned until 1936, when it was sold to the City of Cincinnati for use by the waterworks. The lines ran to branches in California, Batavia, Russellville, Felicity and Bethel but never fulfilled its mission to reach Portsmouth, Ohio. There was also a stop at Coney Island. In 1902, it became one of the first steam railroads in the country to convert to electricity.

A head-on fatal collision between a steam and electric train prompted the forced retirement of all steam service in 1915. Donham Avenue viaduct was having problems and was removed in 1917. The Pennsylvania/Little

Above: Pendleton Railroad Yards connected Cincinnati to many other railroads across the country. *Vickie Rafferty.*

Left: The Carrel Street Memorial recognizes the old railroad station. *Dinese Young*

GRAND OPENING
—OF THE—
EAST END ELECTRIC RAILWAY,
UNDER THE AUSPICES OF THE
EAST END IMPROVEMENT ASSOCIATION.

You are invited to take part in the excursion, etc.
Cars will leave the East End, Thursday Evening, Sep-
tember 3rd, 1891, promptly at 6.30 o'clock.
Bring this with you. as your ticket of admission.

R. H. LANGDALE, }
L. B. ROBB, } *Committee.*

This ticket was for the grand opening of East End Electric Railway. *Carnegie Center of Columbia Tusculum.*

Miami Railroad raised its tracks through Columbia Tusculum, creating overpasses at Delta and Stanley Avenues. Two other rail companies financed construction of a track extension on Kellogg Avenue from Donham to Stanley Avenue, for a new connection to the street railway. Despite the improved connection, by 1918 the rental fees paid to the street railway to allow their California and Coney Island cars to reach downtown had become too expensive, and city service was ended. They continued to operate a few cars to downtown for express freight service, but this was terminated in 1922. The east–west line was dubbed "Thieves Highway" by locals because local thieves in the early 1900s would steal from railcars loaded with goods heading downtown Cincinnati.

With the Victorian boom in Columbia during the late 1800s, there was a larger need for residents in moving around town. The streetcar system helped residents with daily transportation needs in and around the town. In 1866, the Cincinnati and Columbia Street Railway Company began operation of steam "dummies," and in the 1890s, the line was modernized with cable cars. The "dummy" provided a means of getting to Mount Lookout from Columbia and proved to be very popular. The Cincinnati and Columbia Street Railroad ran it along Eastern Avenue and up to Mount Lookout, stopping at St. John's Park. It was so popular that when it ceased operation, a funeral service was held, the cars were cremated and they were buried along Delta Avenue.

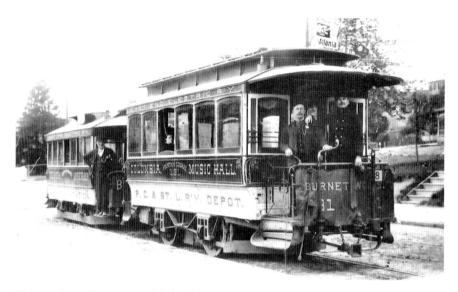

The popular trolley connected Columbia, Music Hall and Fountain Square. *Brian Williams.*

The Cincinnati Traction Railway line was on Donham. *Jonathan P. Scharlock.*

Conductors pose with an East End streetcar. *Brian Williams.*

Cincinnati Traction Railway delivered materials to the stores on Eastern Avenue in the business district. It went under the railroad bridge, where they unloaded supplies for the Heatly Hardware Store on Donham Avenue. A streetcar for passengers also went along Kellogg Avenue, across the railroad tracks, across Eastern Avenue and down Morris Place.

Streetcar motormen, conductors and friends Edward Franz and Harold Barrere lived and worked in the community. Franz went on to a successful career in the trucking business, spending his years at Donham Avenue and the Pennsylvania Railroad. Barrere became the head of Barrere funeral home at 3734 Eastern Avenue.

As early as 1795, a road was surveyed from Cincinnati to Columbia, and by 1835, the Anderson Turnpike was passing through Columbia on its route to Chillicothe. As the population grew, the network of roads connecting towns increased. With the development of the automobile, more people moved out to the suburbs and began to commute to the city for trade and work.

In 1938, Columbia Avenue was upgraded to a parkway to assist in the flow of traffic from the outlying areas into the city. Converting the road into a parkway took seven years of work and $6 million. It continues to provide a direct, high-speed traffic outlet from the downtown district to the eastern suburbs of Cincinnati.

Columbia Parkway looking east from Whittaker Street Foot Bridge after improvements, November 1938. *Brian Williams.*

Another important transportation feature is Lunken Airport. The airport was started as a barnstorming airfield shortly after World War I by a group of ex-army pilots who leveled off some of the grain fields. After Charles Lindbergh's transatlantic solo flight and stop at the airfield, interest in the boom of aviation grew. In 1925, E.H. Lunkenheimer donated 204 acres of ground to the City of Cincinnati to be used as an airport on the condition that it be called Lunken Airport. This donation was added to adjacent purchased land to total 1,004 acres for the airport's development.

In 1925, the U.S. Army Air Corps moved to the present Lunken field. Embry and Riddle formed a team that same year and in 1927 began carrying airmail from Chicago to Cincinnati. Its 4.5-mile distance from downtown Cincinnati made the location convenient for transporting people for business. The Embry-Riddle Company was taken over by American Airlines, making Cincinnati the birthplace of commercial aviation in the United States.

In about the middle of 1928, Lunken became a municipal airport. In the early 1930s, it was known as one of the largest and finest municipal airports in the world. In 1938, the Art Deco terminal building was built

The Edmund Lunken plaque commemorates the airport's land donor. *Carnegie Center of Columbia Tusculum.*

Lunken was the birthplace of American Airlines. *Carnegie Center of Columbia Tusculum.*

Aerial view showing Lunken Airport. *Brian Williams.*

to provide ticketing, managers' offices, the FAA Flight Service Station, a lobby and several business offices. Charles Lindbergh achieved a historic feat, becoming the first person to nonstop fly across the Atlantic Ocean. On August 6, 1927, he landed the *Spirit of St. Louis* at Lunken Airport, concluding a victory tour three months after the notorious journey. Isabella Hopkins, sister of Mariemont founder Mary Emery, announced that Mariemont's Bell Tower would annually ring in celebration of Lindbergh's achievement. The tradition continues today.

In 1947, the Greater Cincinnati Regional Airport, known as CVG, opened as the region's commercial aviation hub. At that point, Lunken Airport began catering to private flyers, non-scheduled commercial cargo ships and executive and corporate aircraft. The airfield provides private, corporate and small business hangars, fixed base operators, aircraft sales and services, air taxi service, sightseeing rides, flight instruction, storage, aviation fuel and oil sales and more.

This ticket counter was inside the Lunken Airport terminal. *Brian Williams.*

In 1963, a control tower, extended runways and installation of Instrument Landing System updated the airport. The opening of Greater Cincinnati Airport brought about the end of major commercial service at Lunken. It is now one of the most important municipal airports in the state and continues to support the industry.

HOUSES OF WORSHIP

Columbia's religious diversity started with early Natives, each tribe having their own practices and beliefs. The religion of the Miami (Myaamia) revolved around a secret religious organization called the Midewiwin, or Grand Medicine Society. Members were thought to have the ability to communicate with spirits and to heal the sick. The Shawnee worshipped both a Great Spirit and the spirits of nature and natural objects such as mountains and animals. They also worshipped a deity known as Our Grandmother, who they believed responsible for creation and for drawing souls up to heaven in a net.

This religious diversity continued with the very first boat of Anglo-American settlers in 1788. Within the small group, there were multiple religions practiced. Therefore, upon settlement and early development of Columbia, multiple churches were quickly established, including Baptist, Presbyterian, Methodist, Catholic and other denominations. Because of the diversity of religions practiced, the small town was home to many beautiful houses of worship, several of which are still standing.

COLUMBIA BAPTIST CHURCH, 3718 EASTERN AVENUE

The original settlers on the boat had six Baptists, one of whom was Benjamin Stites. The first service was held December 1789 in a blockhouse built by Stites, making it the first Protestant church in the Northwest Territory.

The sermon was provided by Reverend David Jones. In 1790, there was a meeting of nine people in the home of Benjamin Davis to organize the Baptist Church. Reverend Steven Gano presided, Isaac Ferris was chosen as deacon and John Gano (brother of pastor and on the first boat) served as clerk. Gano was a surgeon in George Washington's Revolutionary War army. By June of that year, they had eighteen members. Reverend Daniel Clark was the next pastor, but John Smith from Pennsylvania was the first regular pastor. He visited in 1791 but could not start until April 1793.

In 1793, the first church building was constructed on a lot donated by Major Benjamin Stites at the modern-day location of Pioneer Cemetery adjacent to the current Lunken Airport. Before the meeting house was built, meetings were held half of the time at Benjamin Stites's cabin and half of the time at Foster's Bark House. It was used for ten years prior to Ohio becoming a state. The Columbia meeting house was built of hewed logs, two stories high, designed for a gallery (which was never finished), without weather boarding or fireplace. It had a basic pulpit and puncheon seats. In 1811, the exterior was clapboarded. A Corinthian column at the Pioneer Cemetery adjacent to Lunken Airport marks its original location. Reverend Smith spend half of his time preaching downriver in Cincinnati, which didn't have a Baptist church yet, and the other half of his time in Columbia Baptist. In 1793, when he started, there was a congregation of thirty-five people.

In 1794, General Wayne marched forces from Fort Miami up Delta Avenue, cutting a road to Norwood and on to Waynesville. Off this road was the David Jennings farm. Mrs. Jennings, a widow, donated land to build a church in 1801, and they named it Duck Creek. Although no remnants of this church's location or cemetery persist due to the creation of Interstate 71, it was said to be located at the corner of Duck Creek and Edwards Roads.

This "new" church was a replica of the Columbia meeting house but did have a finished gallery and fireplace. Services were held at both Columbia meeting house and Duck Creek. The Duck Creek location was formally changed to Duck Creek Baptist Church in 1827. Over twenty years, many Baptist churches grew out of this location. Two notable and longer running pastors at this Duck Creek church were B.F. Harmon and James Lyon.

In 1798, the Miami Baptist Association forged an alliance with Columbia Baptist, incorporating it into a network of regional Baptist churches. By 1801, Columbia Baptist was seeing a significant increase with more than one hundred new members. Between 1808 and 1865, the congregation convened at Duck Creek Church, constructed in 1803. Services were held in both Duck Creek and the original Columbia Baptist meeting house. Over time, Duck Creek became the primary venue, with Columbia occasionally used for educational purposes. The original Columbia Baptist meeting house endured until 1835 or 1836, when it succumbed to fire. Duck Creek's exact location is not well documented, but one source suggests latitude 39.16527, longitude -84.40791. Unfortunately, both Duck Creek Church

Opposite: The original Declaration of Faith for Columbia Baptist "Books of Church" called John Smith to be first pastor. *Grace and Truth Cincinnati Baptist.*

Right: Name of churches and dates of organization for East Fork Little Miami Baptist Association. Columbia Baptist congregation, renamed Duck Creek, created several branches. *Grace and Truth Cincinnati Baptist.*

Names of Churches and dates of Organization,
of the East Fork Little Miami Association.

- - - - - - - - -

Duck Creek - - - - -1790		Clough- - - - - - - - -1802	
Amelia - - - - - - -1802		East Fork - - - - - - - -1814	
Second Ten Mile - -1819		New Richmond - - - - -1819	
Georgetown - - - -1833		Newtown - - - - - - - -1840	
Bethel - - - - - - -		Stone Lick - - - - - -	
Nicholsville - - - -		Poplar Fork - - - - - -1842	
Withamsville - - - -1845		Clermont Acadamy- - - -1869	
Stone Lick Valley- -1869		New Palestine - - - - -1868	

These names and dates taken from the minutes of the Fifty-Seventh Anniversary of the East Fork Little Miami Association of the Regular Baptists. Held with the Nicholsville Church, Clermont County, Ohio, Saturday September 6, 1873.

In 1816 Duck Creek with seven others, viz: Little Miami, Clover Fork, Clough Creek, Nine Mile, Union, or Indian Creek, Stone Lick, and East Fork Churches were dismissed and formed the East Fork Little Miami Association. **

**(Taken from Miami Baptist History)

and the cemetery were obliterated during the construction of Interstate 71. A second Duck Creek Church arose in 1835, serving the congregation until 1875–76. Relocating to Mount Lookout, it became Duck Creek Baptist of Mount Lookout. In 1904, the congregation moved to Hyde Park as Hyde Park Baptist until 2022. Transitioning to Norwood Baptist in 2022, a satellite of the original Duck Creek Church, they rebranded as Grace and Truth Baptist Church.

Reverend B.F. Harmon served as pastor for thirteen years at Duck Creek and Columbia Baptist, from 1852 to 1865. In 1865, he left and played a key role in establishing Columbia Baptist Church on Eastern Avenue, its present location. His son, Judson Harmon, later became the governor of Ohio. Notably, four members of Columbia Baptist Church—including Isaac Ferris and Benjamin Stites, descendants of original pioneers—founded Columbia Regular Baptist Church of Cincinnati on December 28, 1864, as an offshoot of the Columbia Baptist congregation. The founding members included David, Joseph, Mary, Naomi and Elizabeth Amann; Anna Arthurs; Mary J. Bassett; Anna M. Ferris De Armond; and John M.,

The congregation of Columbia Baptist turned into Duck Creek Baptist. This is Duck Creek Baptist's second location in Mount Lookout on Grace Avenue. *Grace and Truth Cincinnati Baptist.*

Samuel M., William and Mary Ferris. Reverend B.F. Harmon, known for initiating multiple church satellites like Norwood Baptist, assumed the role of pastor, with S.M. Ferris, Dr. E.T. Tibbetts, G.W. Johnston and Charles Stites in leadership positions.

On March 1, 1865, the Council of Churches recognized them as a regular Baptist church, and by September 1865, they had fifty-seven members.

When this group left Duck Creek for Columbia Baptist and Pleasant Ridge Baptist Churches, Duck Creek became so weak in membership that it could barely hold services. During Columbia Baptist's first two years breaking off from Duck Creek, they met in Spenser Town Hall. A lot on Morris Place was purchased for $16,000 to build a new church. It was finished/dedicated on September 29, 1867. The total cost to build the church was $23,000—fully half of which was paid for by four people.

In 1866, a branch was established in Mount Washington, and Reverend Harmon served in both locations. After three years, the Mount Washington church gained independence, transforming into Mount Washington Church. Pastor Harmon led this church, while Reverend M.H. Worrall took charge at Columbia Baptist for two years, succeeded by Reverend W.W. Sawyer for one. Reverend W.E. Stevens, ordained in 1876, held the longest pastorate term in the church's history, spanning over twenty-three years. In 1880, he constructed a house at 3718 Morris Place, situated directly behind the church. Despite Reverend Stevens's popularity, when he resigned on March 21, 1899, seeking work at the state level with Baptist organizations, the church hesitated to accept, given his substantial growth in membership and widespread approval. In 1877, Columbia Baptist congregants in Mount Lookout formed Mount Lookout Baptist. Following a fire, the church was rebuilt in 1894 at a fraction of the original cost.

In 1875, the Duck Creek church moved to Grace Avenue in Mount Lookout due to population shifts and migrations. In 1904, the church began holding meetings and services in the Hyde Park City Hall. On November 6, 1904, the church formally changed its name from Duck Creek Baptist to Hyde Park Baptist. Plans were made to build a church building at the corner of Erie and Michigan Avenues in Hyde Park. The first services were held in the chapel of the new building in July 1901, and the building was dedicated on October 7, 1908. In 1926, the first services were held in the sanctuary of the Hyde Park Building. The Sanctuary and attached business block were dedicated on November 28, 1926. In 2022, the congregation of Hyde Park Baptist Church moved to Norwood, Ohio, and was renamed Grace and Truth Baptist Church.

For the initial forty-five years of Columbia Baptist Church, its doctrine leaned toward conservatism and opposed "book learning." Early church minutes reveal members investigating reports of excessive drinking, "family contentions," absence from church meetings, profanity and marital discord. Instances of excommunication for drinking and swearing are documented. Offending members were called to repent and faced punishment. On March

Columbia Baptist was reestablished on Eastern Avenue. *Brian Williams.*

11, 1793, a church vote led to the suspension of Brother Gano for playing "bawl," thought to be a commoner's term for cricket. Even in July 1861, meeting notes declared dancing as "unbecoming and sinful," warranting excommunication. In 1833, the General Convention of Baptist Western Baptists outlined programs in missions, ministerial education, Sunday schools, religious publications and temperance societies. Columbia Baptist, from its inception, supported abolitionism. Although records lack entries of people of color becoming members until the late 1800s, the church allowed separate services for the community members of color. In the early 1800s, a committee aimed to include such individuals, offering a lecture room for their services but mandating a separate church organization unit until they demonstrated "genuine conversion" for full church membership. Assistance was provided in establishing a separate church for the Black congregants on Columbia Avenue near Delta.

In the mid- to late 1800s, Columbia Baptist collaborated with local churches of different denominations, sharing services and Sunday school. The Methodists, for instance, utilized the building on Sunday afternoons for an extended period. By 1878, the congregation numbered 130, increasing to 169 in 1879, leading to a building expansion that same year. During the floods of 1883 and 1884, Columbia Baptist aided locals facing temporary homelessness, fostering community interest and church membership growth. In 1894, plans were made for a new Columbia Baptist church, and construction, costing less than $14,000, took place during the summer/autumn, with dedication on January 13, 1895. Lots at the rear were sold for $3,425 in 1894. Over the next two years, the congregation expanded to 405 members.

ST. STEPHEN CATHOLIC CHURCH, 3804 EASTERN AVENUE

Early Catholic residents in Columbia undertook arduous journeys to attend services and school at St. Francis DeSales Church in East Walnut Hills or St. Philomena Church in downtown Cincinnati. Although the first recorded mass in Ohio occurred in the Turkey Bottom area by a French missionary traveling the Ohio River, Columbia's Catholic community did not establish its own church until March 3, 1867. The founders petitioned Archbishop Purcell for a distinctly German church and school, exclusively using the German language in mass and school. After they leased a lot from Joseph Longworth for twenty years, the cornerstone was laid by May 19. Parish records indicate significant assistance from Protestants in Columbia during the construction of the first church. Archbishop Purcell blessed the church, completed on November 3, 1867, and named it St. Stephen after the first martyr.

By 1868, a combined school and pastor's residence had been built behind the new church. It was a two-story brick building that had a classroom on the first floor and an apartment for the priest on the second. St. Stephen was assigned its first resident pastor, Reverend Lawrence M. Klawitter, who was newly ordained, on June 1, 1869. In 1873, Reverend Andrew Fabian from France was appointed Klawitter's successor.

The church struggled in the late 1870s and was forced to sell its organ, pastor's residence and furnishings at public auction in 1880. However, the Victorian boom years in Columbia benefited St. Stephen with increasing congregation and success. In 1908, Father Nau was priest, and there were drawings commissioned to build a new church. The original pastor residence and school was at the right of the church at the front of property. It was moved (using mules) to the back of the property to be used as a convent and added on to (new brick façade) in 1913 to make room for the new, larger school building, which is still on the property and used for parish offices.

Opposite, top: The original St. Stephen Church was built in 1867. *St. Stephen Catholic.*

Opposite, bottom: The original church and the "new" (second) school building to the right, after the original structure was moved to the back of the lot, were photographed in 1913. *St. Stephen Catholic.*

Above: This forty-year anniversary photo of St. Stephen was taken in 1907. *St. Stephen Catholic.*

Top: The second St. Stephen Catholic Church was built in 1924. *St. Stephen Catholic.*

Bottom: Interior sanctuary of St. Stephen Church. *St. Stephen Catholic.*

Tragedy struck on January 23, 1922, when a fire in the "boys sacristy" caused irreparable damage to the church building. By March, it was decided to build a new church in the Italian Renaissance style, which was dedicated by Archbishop Moeller on May 18, 1924. The nave painting was first painted on canvas by Carl Zimmerman and then attached to the wall.

The subject depicts the missionary character of the church. After financial struggles during the Depression under twenty-five years of service, Father Meyer retired in 1943. Soon afterward, the church retired its debt and completed extensive renovations, including the additions of its mural and stained-glass windows.

Because of the mid-century neighborhood population decline, the St. Stephen Catholic School was closed in 1972, only five years after St. Stephen celebrated its one-hundred-year anniversary. The moved convent was demolished in 2003. At the time of publishing, St. Stephen Catholic Church still holds regular mass (in English).

CINCINNATI-COLUMBIA PRESBYTERIAN

In 1790, Dr. David Rice and eight individuals established the Cincinnati-Columbia Presbyterian Church, recognized as the region's "Mother Church" by Presbyterians. The church's original design, created a month after Losantiville settlement and surveyed by Israel Ludlow, featured Virginian James Kemper as its inaugural pastor. Kemper, risking wilderness travel through Native territories, served both the Cincinnati and Columbia congregations. During this era, the Ohio territory was embroiled in conflict between the United States and a coalition of Native tribes led by Miami chief Little Turtle. Columbia and Losantiville/Cincinnati settlements, including the church, faced constant conflicts with Natives resisting U.S. claims to the Northwest Territory. Church members were fined for not carrying a rifle to services.

The dual-congregation setup persisted until 1796, when the congregations divided into two independent churches. Covenant First Presbyterian in downtown Cincinnati (currently on Elm Street) and Pleasant Ridge Presbyterian (initially at Duck Creek, then relocated to 5956 Montgomery Road) emerged. Both churches were operational at the time of this publication.

COLUMBIA EVANGELICAL REFORM CHURCH, 4513 EASTERN AVENUE

The oldest standing church in Columbia is the Columbia Evangelical Reform Church, constructed in 1876 by a German congregation originally known

as First German Evangelical Protestant Columbia Church. The church later adopted the name Columbia Evangelical and Reformed Church in the early 1900s, functioning until 1967. The First German Evangelical Protestant denomination originated in 1782 near Pittsburgh, uniting German Lutherans and non-Lutherans, with "evangelical" denoting a non-Catholic church in Germany. Such churches proliferated on both sides of the Ohio River, reaching Cincinnati, Kentucky, Indiana, Illinois, Iowa and Missouri. Adorned with stained glass, each window acknowledges its donor, and the pipe organ dates to 1911. Acquired by a Baptist congregation in the 1970s, they installed a baptismal pool in 1975. While the bell tower endured, the original steeple was absent at the time of publication.

Opposite: Columbia Evangelical Reform Church, located at 4315 Eastern Avenue. *Laura Joppru.*

Above: The original organ is still found inside of Columbia Evangelical Reform Church. *Laura Joppru.*

COLUMBIA METHODIST EPISCOPAL
(ONCE AT THE NORTHWEST CORNER OF DELTA AVENUE AND COLUMBIA AVENUE)

Columbia Methodist Episcopal Church, having occupied a site for about twenty years on Eastern Avenue, in 1893 completed a beautiful new edifice on Columbia Avenue and moved into it with a membership of 160 and a school of 250. Reverend S.G. Pollard was pastor, and Charles Crapsey, E.W. Pettit, Dr. John T. Booth, C.W. Short, Walter Tasker, J.H. Rogers, E.F. Rardon, W.E. Mears and Thomas Dressel were some of the church officers. Built in 1881, Delta Avenue Methodist Church sat at the corner of Columbia Parkway and Delta Avenue. It was one of the buildings in the area designed by Samuel Hannaford & Sons, a very well-known and respected architectural firm that designed buildings such as Cincinnati's Music Hall and Columbia's East End Library.

Built in 1881, Delta Avenue Methodist Church sat at the corner of Columbia Parkway and Delta Avenue. *Nikki Nickell.*

MOUNT CARMEL BAPTIST CHURCH, 3101 RIVERSIDE DRIVE

In 1892, a group of Christians in the East End—including Marshall Smith, Laural Smith, Mary Smith, Porter Oglesby, Mollie Oglesby, Frank Cook, Carrie Cook, Charles Humphries, Sallie Humphries, George Newton and Maggie Newton—started the People's Mission, evolving into the Pendleton Mission and later Mount Carmel Baptist Church. Under Reverend Hockey Smith (1892–1894) and Reverend W. Andrew Jackson (1894–1895), they faced rapid growth, relocating several times before settling at 3101 Eastern Avenue. With Reverend C.M. Thomas (1908) at 2939 Eastern Avenue,

Mount Carmel Baptist Church changed locations multiple times since 1892: 260 Corbin Street, 2939 Eastern Avenue and 3101 Eastern Avenue, as seen in this photo. *Mount Carmel Baptist Church.*

membership surged, necessitating a new facility. Subsequent pastors—including Reverend J. Harden, Reverend J.J. Cummins (1912) and Reverend Robert Watkins (1917–18)—led the church through various locations until Reverend John Thomas Moore (1918–31) secured the GAR Hall on Eastern Avenue and Ridgley Street as the permanent home. Reverend Henry Preston Horne (1932) and Reverend Harold Henderson (1933–34) guided the church through the Great Depression. Reverend Thomas L. Barron (1936–74) provided long-term leadership, followed by Reverend Dr. Donald E. Hamilton (1974–2004) and Reverend Dr. Ashton G. Allen, who led the church at the time of publication. Their current building at 3101 Riverside Drive was constructed in 2002.

COMMUNITY LANDMARKS

ALMS PARK, 710 TUSCULUM AVENUE

Above the historic grounds of Columbia lies Alms Park, nestled among the bluffs once known as Bald Hill, where Native Americans once cleared foliage to monitor the movements of early settlers. Today, this ninety-four-acre expanse, now known as Frederick H. Alms Memorial Park or simply Alms Park, is overseen by the Cincinnati Park Board. Initially gifted to the city by Mrs. Frederick H. Alms in 1916 as a tribute to her late husband, the park occupies land previously owned by Nicholas Longworth, renowned for his Catawba wine production before the Civil War.

Designed in 1929 by Albert D. Taylor, a prominent landscape architect from Cleveland, the park features an eye-catching entrance. Noteworthy attractions include a comfort station erected in 1936 through Works Progress Administration funding and a statue commemorating Stephen Foster Collins, crafted by Arturo Ivone in 1937 and donated by admirer Josiah Kirby Lilly. Facing the Kentucky hills, the memorial pays homage to Foster's songwriting era in Cincinnati, including his famed "My Old Kentucky Home."

Central to the park's allure is the Italian Renaissance–inspired pavilion, a 1929 masterpiece by architects Stanley Matthews and Charles Wilkins Short Jr. Landscape designs by Taylor grace the front terrace and pathways, echoing his work at Ault and Mount Echo Parks. With hiking

East End Café, seen here in 1925, was located at 4003 Eastern Avenue. *Janette Jackson.*

trails, playgrounds and scenic overlooks, Alms Park provides views of Lunken Airport, the Kentucky hills and the confluence of the Little Miami and Ohio Rivers. Benches and shaded retreats are scattered throughout, inviting visitors to enjoy the panoramic beauty.

COLUMBIA CENTER, 3500 COLUMBIA PARKWAY

The building called Columbia Center at Delta Avenue and Columbia Parkway was originally built in 1904 as Yeatman's Masonic Lodge no. 162 and continued as such until 1979, when it moved its lodge to Kellogg Avenue near Lunken Airport. Lodge no. 162 is now located in Mount Washington. J. Michael Smith, Master of Yeatman Lodge, is one of a few original members left who was made a Mason in the original building. Lodge no. 162 sold it in 1979 to an antiques auctioneer. At that time, the lodge rented from Linwood Lodge on Eastern Avenue (now merged with Norwood Lodge). Yeatman merged with Mount Washington Lodge in 1994 and became Yeatman–Mount Washington Lodge no. 162. Gerard Lodge in Newtown merged into Yeatman–Mount Washington Lodge in 2015, and then it reverted to the original name Yeatman Lodge no. 162 F&AM. Yeatman Lodge is named after the first Hamilton County recorder,

Top: The groundbreaking of Yeatman's Lodge. *Junior League of Cincinnati.*

Bottom: Yeatman's Mason Lodge is now occupied by Junior League of Cincinnati. *Junior League of Cincinnati.*

Griffin Yeatman. An original oil painting of Griffin Yeatman is at Mount Washington Lodge, and the copy is at the recorder's office.

The door overlooking today's Columbia Parkway once featured a sizable, ornate stained-glass window, later taken by the Masons to their Lunken Airport site and then moved to the Mount Washington lodge. One of these windows is framed and exhibited. The initial structure at Delta Avenue and Columbia Parkway now houses the Junior League of Cincinnati. Despite various renovations, the original lighting fixtures from the second-floor auditorium are currently in operation on the building's first floor.

East End Library, 3738 Eastern Avenue

Number 3738 Eastern Avenue was one of 1,689 libraries built with money donated by Scottish American businessman and philanthropist Andrew Carnegie in the United States. East End branch library was built in 1906 to the specifications of the noted architectural firm of Samuel Hannaford & Sons, with land donated by the community. It served as a public library until 1959, when it was sold into private use.

During the 1960s and 1970s, the former library housed the Fraternal Order of Police and Veterans of Foreign Wars. In 1994, driven by Columbia Tusculum residents, the vacant building underwent restoration. With

East End Library served the community from 1906 to 1959. *Carnegie Center of Columbia Tusculum.*

backing from neighborhood organizations, individuals, foundations and the City of Cincinnati, the Carnegie Center of Columbia Tusculum emerged as a nonprofit community center. Recognized by the Cincinnati Preservation Association, the nonprofit group received an award for their renovation.

FULTON PRESBYTERIAN CEMETERY, 256 CARREL STREET

Located just five hundred feet from Pioneer Cemetery, Fulton Presbyterian Cemetery sits at the end of present-day Dumont Street along the bike path and was added to the National Historic Register in 1979. Established in 1794, its original ownership or affiliation with a specific church remains unconfirmed. Comprising Fulton Mechanic's Cemetery, Presbyterian Cemetery and Fulton Cemetery, the three adjacent burial grounds share similar dates. There's a possibility that one of these cemeteries was associated with the early Cincinnati–Columbia Presbyterian Church due to the proximity and overlapping timeframes.

The cemetery dates to 1794 and is the final resting place of at least eight Revolutionary War veterans, allegedly including Sergeant Willam Brown, one of two men to receive the first Purple Heart from George Washington. His headstone has not officially been located, possibly due to the removal of

Fulton Presbyterian Cemetery is in the National Register. *Carnegie Center of Columbia Tusculum.*

Fulton Presbyterian Cemetery dates to 1794. *Carnegie Center of Columbia Tusculum.*

headstones during the building of the railroads. It was added to the National Register on August 24, 1979. This site can be seen and accessed off the Ohio River Bike Trail that crosses Carrel Street.

KELLOGG HOUSE, 3807 EASTERN AVENUE

Known as Kellogg House, 3807–11 Eastern Avenue was built in 1835 by Samuel Knicely in Georgian Revival architectural style. Knicely's family was among the original Columbia settlers and came to own most of the land in what is now Columbia Tusculum. Samuel made a living partly from selling pork on the Ohio River and opened an inn and restaurant in the home for river travelers, making the house a center of activity for the village. Samuel's daughter, Sarah, married Ensign Kellogg in 1849 and moved into the house, where they lived and raised their children for fifty years. One of their sons, Edwin, was a city councilman for twenty-one years and lived his entire life in Kellogg House. Three generations of the Kellogg family lived in the home, including Edwin's niece, Mary, until 1977. Numerous members of the Kellogg family resided here. In 1890, Ensign K., Edwin, George, Marshall and Willard listed this as their place of residence. Marshall (1864–1950) was a machinist, George was employed at Shillito's and Willard was a conductor. Ensign Kellogg manufactured bricks in New Richmond.

In 1907, there were extensive Victorian renovations, including the addition of a built-in reed organ and enclosed glassed porch. Also added at

Marshall K. Kellogg and family, September 1892, pose in front of their home on 3711 Eastern Avenue, known as Kellogg House. *Ben and Dinese Young.*

Marshall, Edwin and Sarah pose on the porches of Kellogg House on Sunday, April 19, 1908. *Ben and Dinese Young.*

this time were carved Greek Revival columns in the entry, ornate fireplace mantels, bay windows, Victorian fretwork and iron fencing. In 1979, it was added to the National Register of Historic Places.

LINCOLN SCHOOL, 455 DELTA AVENUE

The Lincoln School was built in 1897 at 455 Delta Avenue in the Romanesque Revival style by architect Henry Siter. This large public school was built to educate up to one thousand neighborhood students; it ceased being a school in the 1980s. Now an office building, it is in the National Register of Historic Places.

MCKINLEY ELEMENTARY, 3905 EASTERN AVENUE

Cincinnati was the first city to have a public school system in the Northwest Territory. Cincinnati Public Schools consolidated several independently operating public schools in 1829 and called itself the Common Schools of Cincinnati. McKinley Elementary was built in 1876 and named after William McKinley, the twenty-fifth United States president, from Niles, Ohio. The building is now occupied by the Irish Heritage Center.

Constructed in 1876 on Tennyson Street, McKinley School reflects Italianate and Jacobethan styles. In the 1890s, H. Siter devised a roof framing plan, and E.H. Dornette oversaw toilet room alterations in

McKinley Elementary was built in 1876. *Carnegie Center of Columbia Tusculum.*

1909. The gymnasium received stage lighting from the Kliegi Brothers Lighting Company of New York. A two-story Eastern Avenue addition was completed in 1919. It was added to the National Register of Historic Places on August 24, 1979.

McKinley was closed as a public school in 2005, when the student population was combined with Linwood Elementary in the new Riverview East Academy. In 2009, the empty school was converted into the Irish American Heritage Center of Cincinnati through the vision and leadership of Maureen Kennedy and Kent Covey. The forty-thousand-square-foot building houses an Irish pub, a theater and concert hall where the Irish American Theatre Company and Celtic musicians perform, a tearoom, a library, a museum, a children's room and a ballroom. The Irish Heritage Center Charitable Foundation's mission is to promote the culture, traditions and story of the Irish and Irish Americans in Greater Cincinnati and Northern Kentucky.

MORRIS HOUSE, 3644 EASTERN AVENUE

Located at 3644 Eastern Avenue, this house stands as the oldest continuously inhabited dwelling in Hamilton County. In the earliest days of Columbia, it was part of one of the largest and most prominent farms in the community. Initially constructed in 1804 as a spacious, multi-room log home, the residence underwent significant modifications and expansions by James C. Morris, renowned as the first manufacturer in Hamilton County due to his

Morris House, located at 3644 Eastern Avenue. *Dinese Young.*

MORRIS HOUSE: A COMPLEX HISTORY

The search for historical records pertaining to the property in Columbia known as Morris House unveiled insights into its ownership history and architectural features. While the quest for a definitive plat map continues, various documents and testimonies shed light on the property's past.

The ownership history of the property has been a subject of meticulous scrutiny. James Morris, a significant figure in the area, is central to the discussion. Records indicate that Morris did not arrive in Columbia until 1806, following his release from North African captivity during the Barbary Wars.

Conflicting accounts exist regarding the year of Morris's arrival, with some sources suggesting 1798, a claim refuted by navy records and the firsthand testimony of Civil War veteran Thompson Morris, James Morris's son.

Real estate records suggest that Morris acquired the property between 1811 and 1819. However, debates persist regarding the existence of a preexisting structure on the land at the time of Morris's purchase, potentially explaining the persistent belief that the core of the current building dates back to 1804.

Two theories regarding the property's ownership lineage have emerged from discussions with experts. One theory suggests a transfer from Symmes to Ephraim Kibbey to Edward Meeks to Morris. Another theory proposes a transfer from Symmes to Colonel Oliver Spencer, to his daughter Dorothy (Mrs. Edward) Meeks and finally to Morris.

Notably, a passage from *Indian Captivity*, published in 1835, describes an old hewed-log house near the foot of a hill, possibly referring to the property in question. If accurate, this account provides evidence supporting the notion that the structure dates to 1804.

An 1834 map delineating the division of Morris's property posthumously depicts the house, referred to as the Morris Homestead, as the sole building in the area, reinforcing the potential historical significance of the property.

Despite historical claims describing the property as a "log house," closer inspection reveals architectural characteristics inconsistent with traditional log cabins. Instead, the structure is identified as a timber-frame house, potentially an early example with hand-hewn timbers reminiscent of early nineteenth-century construction in the Cincinnati area.

Collaboration with preservationists who saved the house in 1982 corroborates the timber-frame nature of the structure, suggesting that it may be more accurately described as a "hewed-log house" rather than a conventional log cabin.

In conclusion, the investigation into the property's ownership history and architectural attributes underscores the complexities inherent in historical research. While challenges persist in reconciling conflicting accounts and interpreting architectural features, continued exploration promises to illuminate complexities of Columbia's past. The search for an elusive plat map remains ongoing, offering the potential to resolve lingering questions and provide a comprehensive understanding of the property's evolution over time.

tannery. Acquiring the property between 1811 and 1819, Morris augmented the original structure, transforming it into its present form. The property's ownership history includes a transfer from Symmes to Colonel Oliver Spencer, who later passed it on to his daughter, Dorothy Meeks, married to Edward Meeks. Ultimately, the house came into the possession of James Morris. Notably, the dwelling experienced numerous renovations, additions and weatherboard coverings during the 1830s, along with seven distinct roof replacements. Remarkably, its construction closely followed that of the famous Kemper log cabin exhibited at the Cincinnati Zoo, being completed just a few months later.

OHIO RIVER LAUNCH CLUB, 100 STRADER AVENUE (OHIO RIVER MILE MARKER 466)

As one of the oldest Yacht Clubs in the country, having been founded in 1898, the Ohio River Yacht Club is also the oldest privately owned and continuously operated boating club on the Ohio River. The boat club was started in 1898 at the foot of Vance Street (OR mile 467.6).

It was at that location for only one year. Because of strong currents at Vance Street, it was moved to the foot of Worth Street (OR mile 466.3), just over a mile upstream. In its early days, ORLC was home to various regattas, including one in 1908 as described in *Power Boating* magazine and *Motorboat* magazine.

Many well-known Cincinnatians have been associated with the Ohio River Launch Club over the years: R.K. LeBlond of LeBlond Machine Tool; Cap Beaty; Frank Katz; the Stegemeyer family; the Graeter family; Robert Dunville, president of W.L.W.; West Shell; Joe Van Loonen; Carlise and Finch of Carlise & Finch; and Michael Comisar, to mention a few. The individual who has the longest membership with ORLC is Mr. Alex Naish of Al Naish Moving and Storage.

POLICE PRECINCT 6, 311 DELTA AVENUE

This structure was built in 1901 as a horse-drawn police patrol house. It helped Cincinnati become only the second city in the United States to have horse-drawn wagon patrols. The horses were kept in the southern end of the building, and the original exterior sliding doors are still

311 Delta Avenue was built in 1901 as a horse-drawn wagon patrol house, making Cincinnati the second city in the nation to provide such a service. *Carnegie Center of Columbia Tusculum.*

present; hay was kept in an upstairs loft. What is now the lobby was office space for the two-officer shifts. The building served as a patrol station until the 1940s and was then turned into storage. In 1979, it was first converted into a restaurant and was then in 1981 purchased by Jeff Ruby and turned into Cincinnati's first fine dining steakhouse. The horse stables were converted into the main dining room, and the hay loft was transformed into a disco club that quickly became the crème de la crème of Cincinnati nightlife in the 1980s.

Columbia's No. 6 station showcases Romanesque style, crafted by architect Samuel Hanford and Sons. Hanford, a Methodist and prolific late 1800s Cincinnati architect, designed more than three hundred buildings, including city hall, Memorial Hall, Music Hall, Cincinnati Club and Columbia's East End Library, now the Carnegie Center of Columbia Tusculum. This building is listed in the National Register of Historic Places. At the time of publication, the Precinct steakhouse is Cincinnati's longest continuously running fine dining restaurant.

PIONEER CEMETERY, 333 WILMER AVENUE

Pioneer Memorial Cemetery, situated on Wilmer Avenue just north of Davis Lane and opposite Lunken Airport, holds a significant place in Hamilton County, Ohio. Recognized as the oldest cemetery in the county, it is known by multiple names, including Columbia Baptist Cemetery, listed in the National Register of Historic Places.

This cemetery serves as the eternal resting ground for a diverse array of individuals, including pioneers, Revolutionary War veterans and Civil War veterans. As the sole restored remnant of the original Columbia settlement dating back to 1788, it holds immense historical importance.

Among its notable features is the earliest gravestone, marking the passing of Phebe Stites, daughter of Hezekiah Stites and niece of Major Benjamin Stites, who died at just five months old in 1797. Additionally, the cemetery's grounds once housed the inaugural Columbia Baptist Church, established in 1790.

A striking Corinthian pillar, once part of a local post office, now stands as a memorial to the pioneering spirits who shaped the region, having been relocated to the cemetery where it stands as a testament to their legacy. It is one of six columns that stood in front of the old post office located downtown Cincinnati at Fourth and Vine Streets between 1856

Pioneer Cemetery, where the original settlers are buried, was deeded to the Cincinnati Parks Department in 1937 by Cincinnati Baptist Church Union. *Linda Wedding*

and 1885. Throughout its history, the cemetery has witnessed periods of care and neglect. In the early 1900s, Russell Stites and others undertook its upkeep, with annual Memorial Day parades organized by local schoolchildren to honor the veterans interred within. In 1923, a marker commemorating Major Benjamin Stites was erected, reaffirming his pivotal role in founding Columbia.

Despite it being donated to the city of Cincinnati in 1937 to establish a Memorial Pioneer Cemetery, neglect crept in until 1967, when Frederick Payne spearheaded a restoration effort, culminating in the preservation of invaluable historical records now housed at the Cincinnati Historical Society.

Moreover, the cemetery's significance extends beyond its colonial-era origins. In 1958, it was revealed to sit atop the remnants of a Native American village from the Woodland Mound period, preserving this archaeological site from excavation. Recent efforts by organizations like the National Association for Black Veterans Chapter no. 68 and the My GI Foundation have honored Black veterans buried between 1790 and 1867, adding new headstones and a monument in 2019.

"Columbia Settlement: 1788 Revisited" is a living history event celebrating Cincinnati's very first settlement. The event originally included a walking tour of the cemetery but now takes place at Sharon Woods' Heritage Village Museum. Visitors hear from people of the past (interpreters in period dress) about their lives and about the people who are buried in the cemetery, as well as others who lived in the Columbia Settlement area from the late 1700s to the early 1800s.

SPENCER TOWNSHIP HALL, 3833 EASTERN AVENUE

Formerly the Spencer Township government seat before annexation by Cincinnati, Spencer Township Hall is named in honor of Colonel Spencer, an early Columbia settler and father of Reverend Oliver M. Spencer. The reverend's captivating account of Indian captivity offers detailed insights into the late 1700s local Native American life. Originally the meeting place for the Independent Order of Odd Fellows Lodge, the Greek Revival–style two-story brick building was constructed in 1860. Recognized in the National Register of Historic Places since 1979, it owes its listing primarily to its architectural significance.

Left: Spencer Township Hall was originally the seat of government for Spencer Township. *Dinese Young.*

Below: Little Miami River bottom, once known as Turkey Bottom, was developed into Lunken Airport. *Grace and Truth Cincinnati Baptist.*

Turkey Bottoms, Along Little Miami River

The banks of the Little Miami River at present-day Lunken Airport hold significant historical importance in southwest Ohio, dating back to ancient Native settlements and the region's first American settlement in 1788. The burial grounds of settlers, Native Americans and ancient mound builders lie beneath the modern runways. While the land for the airport was prepared, several Native American items were unearthed. The area had previously been a Native burial ground and contained numerous items of artifacts such as arrowheads, tomahawks and pottery. The rich soil provided for a bountiful corn crop for the Native Americans and later the settlers.

The area, originally known as Turkey Bottoms, featured fertile alluvial soil that made it a crucial granary and trade center. Pioneers bestowed the name Turkey Bottoms due to the abundance of wild turkeys in the river bottom; it was joked that there were so many turkeys in this area that one could hunt a turkey just standing in their front door waiting.

As a flourishing grain farm region, Turkey Bottom yielded one hundred baskets of corn per acre, leading to the development of local mills and distilleries in the late 1790s. The earliest gristmill was established in 1796 by Jacob Wikersham. Acquired by Philip Turpin in 1822, Turpin's Mill operated until 1868 and was later demolished in 1870.

In addition to the Native American remains, an old stone from the early gristmill on the site was uncovered. The preserved millstone from Turpin's Mill is displayed near the west entrance of Lunken Airport's Administration Building, offering visitors a glimpse into the area's rich history.

Stephen Decker Row Houses, 531–41 Tusculum Avenue

This multiple-residence Victorian townhouse is in the National Register of Historic Places due to its exemplary preservation of Victorian architecture and is the only remaining townhouse of its kind in Cincinnati. It was built in 1889 on land that was once part of Nicholas Longworth's extensive and successful vineyards. Located at 531–41 Tusculum Avenue, the Stick-style Victorian row house was built with step construction and Gothic weather boarding.

STITES HOUSE, 315 STITES AVENUE

Constructed in 1835 by Hezekiah Stites Jr., the Stites House on 315 Stites Avenue, Columbia, remains a testament to the family's longevity in the community. The back section, added in 1867 by Charles Stites, contributes to the structure's enduring quality. With eighteen-inch-thick masonry walls, the brick house exhibits a blend of Federal and Greek Revival styles, boasting a stone foundation and shingled roof. Listed in the National Register of Historic Places, this residence preserves its early nineteenth-century charm to this day.

VERDIN BELL FACTORY, 3900 KELLOGG AVENUE

Verdin Bell Company is the oldest family-owned business in Ohio and one of America's oldest family manufacturing companies. Its factory is in Columbia Tusculum. French immigrant brothers Francis de Sales and Michael Verdin started the Verdin Bell Company in 1842 when they installed the first tower clock in the United States in Old St. Mary's Church. The company has manufactured bronze bells, clocks, towers and even organs for six generations and grew into an industry leader. In 1927, the Verdin company built the first electric bell ringer in America and, in 1999, cast the largest swinging cast bell in America: the World Peace Bell in Newport, Kentucky. In celebration of Ohio's bicentennial, Verdin created the only mobile bell foundry in the world.

NOTABLE PEOPLE

Many prominent Cincinnati figures resided in the Columbia neighborhood, including Councilman Edward Kellogg, Mayor George Carrel, Sheriff C. Taylor Handman (who lived on Morris Place) and his father, Charles Handman, who organized Columbia's YMCA. Harry Damm was a violinist with the Cincinnati Symphony Orchestra, and his family was one of the earliest and largest landowners in the area, whose sheepskin deed was signed by George Washington. Throughout the community's years, Columbia residents contributed to the social and economic fabric of the Queen City.

LARZ ANDERSON

The son of Nicholas Longworth Anderson and Elizabeth Coles Kilgour Anderson, Larz Anderson III was born in Paris, France, on August 15, 1866, and passed away in White Sulphur Spring, West Virginia, on April 13, 1937. He held prominence as a wealthy American businessman and diplomat, briefly assuming the role of U.S. ambassador to Japan from 1912 to 1913. Larz entered the world during his parents' eighteen-month honeymoon in Paris, coinciding with their marriage on March 28, 1865, in Cincinnati, Ohio. Active in esteemed organizations like the Sons of the Revolution, the Loyal Legion and the Society of the Cincinnati, Larz Anderson left a legacy, with Anderson House, the national headquarters of the Society of the Cincinnati in Washington, D.C., being named in his honor. Additionally, a park dedicated to him in Columbia Tusculum was established by 1933 when his widow, Emma Anderson, donated 6.2 acres to the Cincinnati Park Board.

SERGEANT WILLIAM BROWN

Early Columbia pioneer Sergeant William Brown was one of the first two recipients of what is now known as the Purple Heart, the prestigious military decoration created by George Washington, commander in chief of the Continental army on August 7, 1782. This created what is now the oldest decoration for military valor on the battlefield except the Cross of St. George of Russia and the first honor badge for distinguished military service for enlisted and noncommissioned officers in the U.S. Army.

Connecticut-born William Brown had just turned sixteen years old when he enlisted in the Continental army as a member of Captain Samuel Comstock's Company of the Eighth Regiment, Connecticut Line. He served under General McDougall, fighting in Germantown and Battle of Monmouth and encamping at Valley Forge, White Plains and Redding. He rapidly ascended to the level of corporal in 1779, at which time he was stationed on the east side of the Hudson River. General Gorge Washington created a plan to storm Stony Point in which General Anthony Wayne and some brave Connecticut boys were picked to join Meig's Light Regiment for an operation that took place on July 15, 1779. He was awarded his first military medal for bravery during the mission.

One year later, he was promoted to sergeant on August 1, 1780, after which he led a select group of a dozen of the bravest Patriot soldiers during the Siege of Yorktown in an operation called "Forlorn Hope." He was only twenty years old on the night of October 14, 1781, when he was wounded carrying out the assault. Because it was widely viewed as a suicide mission, the resounding success of Sergeant Brown's achievement won him admiration and praise among his brothers in arms. A board of five officers chosen by General Washington passed on candidates for the Badge of Merit, Washington's newly created military award. In the recommendation, the board stated:

> 2d. Serjeant Brown, of the late 5th Connecticut Regiment, in the assault
> of the Enemy's left Redoubt at Yorktown, in Virginia, on 5th evening of

A landmark recognizing Sergeant William Brown, located near Fulton Cemetery. *Dinese Young*

the 14th of October 1781, conducted a forlorn hope with great bravery, propriety and deliberate firmness, and that his general character appears unexceptionable.

The original Purple Heart (Badge of Military Merit) was made of dull purple woolen material in the shape of a heart embroidered with the word *Merit* wreathed in a vine of leaves.

After six years in military service, William Brown returned to Connecticut and married his cousin Ruth Hanford. Several young Revolutionary War veterans were enticed to cheap western lands opened to settlement in the Northwest Territory, especially since "Mad Anthony Wayne," under whom they served with devotion in the war, was said to be taking charge of military forces in the territory. In the spring of 1793, now President George Washington sent General Anthony Wayne to Cincinnati to subdue the Native Americans, at which time Wayne immediately called on Brown to provide a group of spies. This group of veterans were excited to serve Wayne once again.

REVEREND STEPHEN GANO

Reverend Stephen Gano was part of the original settlers who founded the Baptist Church of Columbia in 1790 and presided over the meeting establishing the church. Gano was a surgeon in George Washington's Revolutionary War army.

PIGMEAT JARRETT

James "Pigmeat" Jarrett (1899–1995), a barrelhouse blues pianist and singer of Geechee descent, made a lasting impact on Cincinnati's blues scene. Jarrett was born in Georgia, and his family moved to Kentucky and eventually settled in the Columbia neighborhood, where he learned blues piano at local gatherings. Playing during the Prohibition era, he left a significant mark on the city's piano blues sound. After a hiatus in the 1940s, Jarrett was rediscovered in his elder years, recording his only studio album in 1979. He performed at major blues festivals and secured a regular gig at Arnold's Grill in Cincinnati until his death at the age of ninety-five on September 5, 1995. Despite being recorded only once, Pigmeat Jarrett's contributions to the blues genre, his unique style and enduring influence on Cincinnati's music scene are celebrated aspects of his legacy.

HERSHEL JOINER

Hershel Joiner (1917–1996) was a community resident who lived on both Ridgley and Walworth. He fought as a boxer from 1937 to 1946, was five-foot-nine and had a record of 24-18-4, with 16 wins by knockout. He won featherweight, lightweight and welterweight state champion titles. He was

Left: Reverend Stephen Gano had careers in both medicine and ministry. *Grace and Truth Cincinnati Baptist.*

Right: John Stites Gano was one of the pioneers at Columbia and fought in the War of 1812. *Grace and Truth Cincinnati Baptist.*

Pigmeat Jarrett played live every Wednesday night at Allyn's Café in his later years. *Allyn Raifstanger.*

William Hershel Joiner was one of only two boxers who defeated featherweight champion and Hall of Famer Freddie Miller, in 1940. *Brian Williams.*

the uncle of heavyweight Billy Joiner. Hershel lost in the semifinals of the 1937 National AAU Tournament in Boston to Charley Miele of Lincoln, Nevada, in the featherweight class. He was married to Eva Evelyn and had one child.

EDWIN KELLOGG

Edwin Kellogg, born to Ensign Kellogg and Sarah Knicely, who was the daughter of Samuel Knicely, responsible for constructing the residence at 3807 Eastern Avenue, hailed from the original Columbia settlers. Throughout his entire life, Edwin resided in this home until his passing at the age of seventy-five. His political journey commenced in 1885 when he secured a clerkship at the City Engineer's Office. Subsequently, he dedicated twenty-one years to serving on the Cincinnati City Council from 1899 onward. During his tenure, Edwin vigorously advocated for numerous community enhancements. Notable projects he championed included the sponsorship of Observatory Avenue, Grandin Road and the Delta Avenue viaduct. He also played a

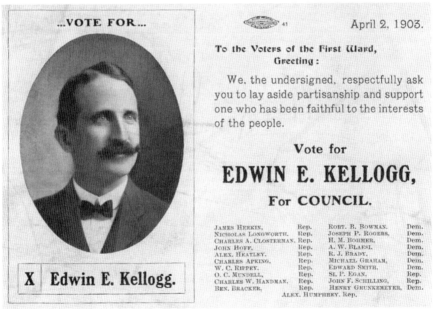

Top: Edwin Kellogg, May 1906. *Ben and Dinese Young*

Bottom: Resident Edwin Kellogg successfully campaigned for the city council in 1903. *Ben and Dinese Young*

pivotal role in the construction of the Kellogg Avenue bridge spanning the Little Miami River, the establishment of a sewage system for Columbia/ East End and the improvement of Eastern Avenue and Linwood Road. Additionally, he sponsored the elevation of Eastern Avenue railroad crossings at Rookwood and Delta Avenues. In honor of his significant contributions, Kellogg Avenue was named after Edwin Kellogg. His legacy endures as a respected city councilman and valued member of the community.

NICHOLAS LONGWORTH

Nicholas Longworth arrived in Cincinnati in 1803 as an eager twenty-one-year-old pioneer. He practiced law until 1819 to focus on real estate. He was phenomenally successful and became Cincinnati's first millionaire. It was said of Longworth, "You couldn't throw that man into the Ohio River without his coming to the surface with a rare species of fish in one hand and a fresh-water pearl in the other." He married Susan Howell Connor, daughter of one of the largest landowners in the Tusculum Hill area of what is now Alms Park. Wine from the grapes he grew in Tusculum and the surrounding areas was so dry and delicate that it rivaled costly champagnes of Europe. The success of his vineyards is what in part drew Germans to the area, as vintners from the Rhine provinces flocked to tend Longworth's vineyards. Longworth became a local philanthropist and supporter of the vibrant Cincinnati arts community.

RUTH LYONS

Ruth Lyons entered the world in Columbia at a time when it was known as the East End and gained acclaim as a renowned local broadcaster and businesswoman. She achieved fame through her widely loved radio and television programs, including the *50-50 Club* and her charitable initiative, the Ruth Lyons Fund. A trailblazer in the TV talk show genre, Ruth innovatively directed the camera toward the audience during filming. Her influence extended to notable broadcasters like Nick Clooney, Bob Braun, David Letterman and Jane Pauley. In 1958, she made a notable appearance on NBC's *Today Show* for a week. Ruth resided locally at 332 Tusculum Avenue and 3614 Morris Place, while her first husband, John, lived at 420 and 427 Tusculum Avenue. The couple exchanged vows at the Morris Place residence.

Ruth Lyons's Ohio Historical Marker can be found at Columbia Square. *Dinese Young*

REVEREND JOHN SMITH

Early settler John Smith became the first full-time pastor at Columbia Baptist Church. In addition to his pastoral duties, Reverend John Smith was an active leader and landowner in the community. He was a wealthy businessman who owned a general store and a large farm. He had a lucrative business selling supplies to the army in Fort Washington, as well as throughout Kentucky and the Northwest Territory. He brought European goods down the Ohio River and stored them in his one room warehouse by the river.

In later years, "Elder Smith," as he was known, owned a house in Terrace Park known as Round Bottom Mills. He was a leading proponent for Ohio's statehood, a member of the first Territorial Assembly in 1798 and Ohio's first U.S. senator, serving in that capacity from 1803 until 1808. During that

LOCAL HERO'S CONNECTION TO INFAMOUS TRAITOR

During John Smith's term as a U.S. senator, Aaron Burr simultaneously held the roles of vice president and president of the Senate. It was during this time that the two formed a close bond, a relationship that persisted even after Burr's infamous duel with Alexander Hamilton. Despite Burr's subsequent political downfall, he plotted against the United States in a scheme aimed at seizing land within the Louisiana Purchase by plotting a rebellion. Burr's ambition was to claim territory for himself, with Harman Blennerhassett of Marietta, Ohio, serving as his main financial backer. Throughout the planning stages, Burr frequently traveled along the Ohio River, often staying as a guest in John Smith's home.

It was never clear whether Smith supported the conspiracy, but he did distribute funds to participants for Burr and shielded Burr's whereabouts. Additionally, Smith's sons engaged with Burr during the plotting phase. However, correspondence between Smith and Burr revealed Smith's apparent ignorance of the conspiracy's true nature, with Burr vehemently denying any involvement.

Despite a failed attempt led by John Quincy Adams to remove him from the Senate by trial, Smith resigned voluntarily amid disgrace. His resignation, sent to Thomas Kirker, acting governor of Ohio, on April 25, 1808, marked the beginning of a period of financial ruin for Smith. The U.S. War Department's outstanding debts amounting to $30,000 for ammunition provisions to the army resulted in the forfeiture of fifteen thousand acres of his land in Ohio. Smith relocated to his Louisiana property, where he resumed his teaching and preaching, albeit amid personal tragedy, losing his wife and all but one of his adult children within a short timeframe.

time, he became a friend and advisor to President Thomas Jefferson. After becoming entangled in the wrong side of the Aaron Burr controversy, he had to sell his land in 1808 when he lost his fortune.

In Cincinnati, Smith's legacy endures through two streets named in his honor: Smith Street, located west of the Clay Wade Bailey Bridge ramp, and John Street, stretching from Court north to York in the West End.

BENJAMIN STITES

Benjamin Stites II, born in 1734, played a significant role in the American Revolution as captain in the Pennsylvania Militia. After his military service, he explored the fertile lands along the Ohio River and, in 1788, founded the town of Columbia in Hamilton County, Ohio. He was an important leader and landowner in the community. Married to Rachel, Benjamin had in a tumultuous relationship, resulting in separation in 1786 with accusations of adultery. His legal children with Rachel included John, Benjamin III, Phebe, Richard and Rachel. However, Benjamin also had children out of wedlock with Mary "Polly" Mills and Hannah Waring. He died in 1804, and his estate was managed by his son Benjamin III, son-in-law James Miranda and Ephraim Kibby, with the children from the illegitimate relationships not considered legatees.

A NEW MILLENNIUM

The early twenty-first century brought renewed interest in urban living, which coincided with the desire for lifestyle changes including shorter commuting times for work, accessibility to cultural and social enrichments, reduced gas expenditures and desire for more recreational and family time. This has benefited urban neighborhoods like Columbia Tusculum. Cincinnati has a total of forty-six neighborhoods, and Columbia Tusculum is one of the most convenient locations on the east side of the city.

The community boundaries of Columbia have changed over time, and modern-day Columbia Tusculum's boundaries are separate and distinct from East End and Linwood. Many old-timers still refer to the entire area inaccurately as "East End." According to the most current bylaws of Columbia Tusculum Community Council at the time of publication, the community boundaries are defined as follows:

> The Columbia Tusculum area is defined as generally bounded on the west by Delta Avenue south of Kleybolte Avenue, and those streets having access only to Delta Avenue; on the north by the south side of Kroger Avenue, Vineyard Place, the south side of Grandin up to and including Catawba Valley Drive and Tusculum Avenue including streets only with access from Tusculum; on the east by Alms Park and Wortman Avenue; and on the south by Eastern Avenue, Airport Road, Wilmer Avenue and the Ohio River.

Some of these boundaries have been disputed by adjacent community councils, such as the inclusion of Walworth and Golden Avenues.

As the first quarter of the twenty-first century concludes, a national housing affordability crisis has hit Americans, especially the young adult generation trying to get their footing in permanent housing. Additionally, after the COVID-19 pandemic of 2020 and 2021, many jobs remained at least partly remote, allowing people greater choice in where they chose to live. Recent research suggests Millennials and Gen Z preferences for living in vibrant cities over rural towns or large suburbs. In 2024, Cincinnati's housing costs were 19 percent lower and cost of living 4 percent lower than the national average, making it appealing to this demographic.

The Greater Cincinnati area ranked fifth on *Forbes'* 2023 list of the ten best places to live for young professionals in America. With Fortune 500 businesses like Proctor & Gamble, Kroger, Fifth Third Bank, Western and Southern Financial, Fidelity Investments and Cintas, Cincinnati has an appealing white-collar job market while having a notably lower cost of living compared to other major U.S. cities. According to the 2020 census, the median age of Columbia Tusculum residents was thirty-four years old, reflecting the neighborhood's appeal to young professionals. According to a 2024 Zillow report, Cincinnati, Cleveland and Columbus were among the ten hottest housing markets in the nation, reflecting the interest in these affordable Ohio cities, which makes sense considering Ohio has the ninth-lowest state tax rate in the United States. Cincinnati was ranked number two, reflecting the very active housing market and desire to live in the city.

In addition to affordability, Cincinnati has the cultural and social resources that make a city desirable. The city has always had a robust arts culture, with professional ballet, the second-oldest opera company in the country, one of the oldest art museums in the country, a renowned symphony, multiple theatrical companies (including Tony Award–winning Playhouse in the Park), many live concert venues and more. Artswave is the nation's oldest and largest united arts fund, and it supports more than 150 organizations providing thousands of arts performances, concerts, programming, exhibitions, public art projects and more. For sports enthusiasts, Cincinnati is home to three professional sports teams: Cincinnati Reds baseball, Bengals football and FC Cincinnati soccer. Additionally, competitive teams at Xavier University and the University of Cincinnati provide exciting college sports events. Just minutes away from these venues and connected by public transit, Columbia Tusculum continues its history of offering convenient accessibility to the best recreation Cincinnati has to offer and appeals to people looking for accessibility to active urban life.

To meet the interest and demand for more urban housing, the City of Cincinnati expanded its tax abatement program to encourage new construction and renovations to existing properties. The Cincinnati Residential Tax Abatement program reduces the amount of property taxes that owners must pay on new construction or improvements to their dwelling for up to fifteen years. In 2023, tax abatements were expanded to include renovations that increase the value of the structure for improvements that are Leadership in Energy and Environmental Design (LEED) Certified, Home Energy Ratings System (HERS) Qualified and multi-family residences. The Columbia Tusculum neighborhood qualifies for these tax abatement programs. Initiatives like this have fueled new construction. Between 2000 and 2020, 106 new buildings were added to the community. Considering 239 out of the 684 households in 2020 were built prior to 1939, this growth demonstrates that Columbia Tusculum is not only a community of historic homes but has ample modern residences as well, with momentum for further development.

Like every other phase of the community's existence, Columbia Tusculum's demographic composition continues to change and evolve with fluctuations and in resident migration. In 2024, the City of Cincinnati recorded the number of Columbia Tusculum residents at 3,198, 91 percent of whom are white and 16.8 percent of whom are children. Most residences are owner-occupied, while 36.5 percent are rentals. Only 4.6 percent of residents live in poverty, and a slight majority have college degrees (52 percent). The median income of community members is $113,194, which is triple the national average. In 2020, the median home value was $373,000, and all homes were valued at $125,000 or greater.

The community's evolution and progression through time remain as consistent as the rapid waters flowing down the Ohio River. Its journey is dynamic and ever changing. Like a steamboat captain, local organizations and community leaders keep the neighborhood on course like a boat on the currents of time. At the time of publication, local nonprofit organizations such as the Columbia Tusculum Community Council, 3 East Business Association, the Carnegie Center of Columbia Tusculum and the Irish Heritage Center are the stewards of Columbia Tusculum, with resident volunteers in management. Since at least 1788, residents have been the life force driving the community's vitality and connectivity.

BIBLIOGRAPHY

American Baptist. "Meet OBC's Oldest Churches." Ohio News Section, February 1976.

Cincinnati Historical Society. "200 Years of Cincinnati." 1988.

Cincinnati Preservation Association. "Preserving Places that Matter." http://www.cincinnatipreservation.org.

City of Cincinnati. "Columbia Tusculum 2020 Statistical Neighborhood Approximation." https://www.cincinnati-oh.gov/sites/planning/assets/2020CENSUS/ColumbiaTusculum_2020.pdf.

"The Columbia Baptist Church: Golden Jubilee, 1865–1915." Pamphlet. Cincinnati Historical Society, Cincinnati, Ohio, 10-3-8, October 1915.

Columbia Tusculum, Cincinnati, Ohio Demographics. U.S. Census Bureau. 2021 American Community Survey. https://www.point2homes.com/US/Neighborhood/OH/Cincinnati/Columbia-Tusculum-Demographics.html.

Columbia Tusculum Community Council. "Columbia Tusculum Community Council Bylaws." June 20, 2016.

Conteur. "Early Settlers in Columbia." *Cincinnati Enquirer*, November 28, 1920.

Dickorie, Marie, ed. "The Fulton Cemeteries in Present Day Cincinnati." Genealogy Department: Cemetery Inscriptions and Biographies. Cincinnati History Library and Archives, Hamilton County, Ohio.

Dodge, J.R. *Red Men of the Ohio Valley: An Aboriginal History*. Springfield, OH: Ruralist Publishing Company, 1860.

Drozdz, Maya. "Pioneer Memorial Cemetery: A Site of Intertwined Histories." Cincinnati Preservation Association. http://www.cincinnatipreservation.org.

Engeleken, Ruth. "The Old Stites House." *Cincinnati Enquirer Magazine* (August 16, 1970).

Ford, Henry A., and Kate B. Ford. *History of Hamilton County, Ohio*. Cleveland, OH: L.A. Williams and Company, 1881.

General Map of the River Ohio. Plate the Third. 1797. Cincinnati History Library and Archives, 977 c714.

Heidler, Robert. "East End-Tusculum." *Cincinnati Times-Star*, August 12, 1950.

Howe, Henry. *Historical Collections of Ohio*. Cincinnati, OH: Laning Company, 1898.

———. *Historical Collections of Ohio in Three Volumes*. Ohio Centennial ed. Columbus, OH: Henry Howe and Son, 1891, circa 1888–91.

Knoop, Mary Ann, et al. *Columbia Tusculum, 1788–1988*. Columbia, OH: Columbia Tusculum Community, 1988.

Medintz, Joshua. "Forbes Ranks Cincinnati, Columbus as Top 5 Metros for Young Professionals." *Cincinnati Enquirer*, July 31, 2023.

Morsbach, Mabel. *We Live in Cincinnati*. Cincinnati Public Schools, 1961.

Ohio Writer's Project. "Tales of Old Cincinnati." Work Projects Administration, 1940.

Papers of the Northwest Territory. "At the Blockhouse Near Columbia." A letter from Benjamin Stites to Governor Arthur St. Clair, April 8, 1789. Library of Congress, Manuscript Division.

Pitcher, M. Avis. "John Smith, First Senator from Ohio and His Connections with Aaron Burr." *Ohio History Journal* 45, no. 1 (January 1936): 68–88.

Putnam, Rufus. *Indians of North America*. Columbus: State of Ohio, 1804. Reproduction, 1966.

Sons of the American Revolution. Interview notes. Archived. Cincinnati History Library and Archives. Cincinnati, Ohio.

Stites, Benjamin. Cincinnati History Library and Archives, MSSVF 2228 q58622.

———. Letter to Governor Arthur St. Clair, April 8, 1789. Cincinnati History Library and Archives, MSSUF 3244.

Strome, Lulu Anna (Gerard). Cincinnati History Library and Archives, MSSUF 2241 q5921.

Symmes, John Cleves. Miami Land Warrant #1, December 17, 1787. Cincinnati History Library and Archives.

———. Photocopy of Miami Land Purchase: Land Warrant #50, April 30, 1788. Cincinnati History Library and Archives, MSSVF 441.

White, John H., Jr. "By Steam Car to Mount Lookout: The Columbia and Cincinnati Street Railroad." *Bulletin of the Cincinnati Historical Society* 25, no. 2 (April 1967).

Williams, Harriet Langdon. "Memory Pictures." Brooklyn, NY: Annie Morrill Smith, 1908. Published for private use.

Wilson, Steven Douglas. "The Adjustment Process of Southern Appalachian Whites in Cincinnati." University of Kentucky ProQuest Dissertations and Theses, 1983.

ABOUT THE AUTHOR

Dinese Young, originally from Columbus, Indiana, relocated to Cincinnati after receiving advanced degrees in education from both Miami University and the University of Cincinnati. She became executive director at the Carnegie Center of Columbia Tusculum in 2012 and spearheaded the reorganization of the nonprofit community center into an arts and cultural resource for Cincinnati's oldest neighborhood. In 2020, she created the Columbia Tusculum Historical Society to preserve and share community history and artifacts. Dinese and her husband purchased their first home in Columbia Tusculum in 1999, and they've since renovated four historic homes, raised children and actively participated in community endeavors.

While teaching fourth-grade history, Mrs. Young taught about the first Cincinnati settlement of Columbia prior to living in the neighborhood. Later, as an active community resident and volunteer, she brought that knowledge and passion about the community's history into many projects. Through years of active volunteering and leadership, her passion for education and historic preservation inspired her to write this book sharing the rich history of "Cincinnati's Oldest Neighborhood" with a wider audience.